THE MYTH OF COACHING MANAGER

Dr Gilbert NG

INDIA • SINGAPORE • MALAYSIA

Copyright © Dr Gilbert NG 2025
All Rights Reserved.

ISBN 979-8-89744-882-1

This book has been published with all efforts taken to make the material error-free after the consent of the author. However, the author and the publisher do not assume and hereby disclaim any liability to any party for any loss, damage, or disruption caused by errors or omissions, whether such errors or omissions result from negligence, accident, or any other cause.

While every effort has been made to avoid any mistake or omission, this publication is being sold on the condition and understanding that neither the author nor the publishers or printers would be liable in any manner to any person by reason of any mistake or omission in this publication or for any action taken or omitted to be taken or advice rendered or accepted on the basis of this work. For any defect in printing or binding the publishers will be liable only to replace the defective copy by another copy of this work then available.

Contents

Contents

List of Tables

List of Figures

Acknowledgements

At this very emotional moment, I cannot imagine finishing my second book without the guidance of my mentor, help from my friends, and support from my family members.

I would like to take this opportunity to thank my family and friends for all the emotional support provided to me. Their support was instrumental in motivating me to carry on to the end of this journey.

Throughout my research, I encountered several obstacles when juggling work commitments and other challenges. It was almost impossible to believe I had made it through my journey. During these difficult times, words of encouragement and comfort from my family and friends kept me moving forward. No better words can adequately express the depth of my appreciation and gratitude than these.

I would also like to personally thank my mentor, Mr. Yeoh Koay Kheng for providing me with all the necessary guidance to successfully complete this research. His encouragement and understanding were helpful to the research, writing and completion of this book.

Dr Gilbert Ng
23rd Jan 2025

Abbreviation

Abbreviation	Description
CEO	Chief Executive Officer
CMO	Chief Marketing Officer
COO	Chief Operation Officer
F&B	Food and Beverage
MCAR	Missing Completely at Random
MNC	Multinational Corporation
SMEs	Small and Medium-sized Enterprises
SPSS	Statistical Package for Social Science
N	Sample Size
VIF	Variance Inflation Factor
WFH	Work from home

Abstract

Coaching is one of the most effective talent strategies because it ensures that talented employees will develop their skills to remain competitive and prevent "Great Resignation". However, modern managers no longer know what needs to be done, teach others how to do it, and evaluate their performance, with a limited understanding of their intention to implement coaching. This study aims to identify the factors which influence the intention to implement manager coaching that will contribute to improving leadership practices in managing "Talent Retention Strategies" for private sector enterprises in Malaysia.

A quantitative study was conducted using online surveys via email, Facebook Messenger, WeChat and WhatsApp to approach the respondents from private sector enterprises, including small and medium-sized Enterprises (SMEs) in Malaysia.

Using the purposive sampling technique, a total of 300 questionnaires were distributed, with 204 questionnaires coded and usable for analysis. Data were analyzed using IBM SPSS 26 software program. Data screening and preparation was conducted to eliminate missing values and outliers in the data collected.

This study examines the factors of these independent variables (e.g., salary, benefits and compensation, work environment, employee engagement, leadership style, as well as training and development) and dependent variable (intention to implement modern's coaching skill). In this study, the empirical results drawn from the multiple regression analysis revealed that leadership style, and training and development are positively and directly influence on managers to implement coaching to retain talent. However, salary, benefits and compensation, work environment and employee engagement have no significant influence on intention to implement modern manager's coaching skill. Therefore, if any company has a great leadership culture and an effective training and coaching framework, their managers are more willing to be a coach. Most companies still have a mismatched ideology that salary, work environment and employee engagement would influence their managers to coach.

This study highlights the significant factors that influence intention to implement coaching skill among the general management position and above in private enterprises in Malaysia. The results of this study could provide useful information for scholars and practitioners. The theoretical contributions highlight how the study of intention to implement coaching contributes to the body of knowledge in management. The study also bestows an understanding of the factors that influence intention to implement for organization to act and improve the talent retention.

CHAPTER 01:

Introduction

1.1   Introduction and Title of Study

Talent Management as a key component to organizational leaders to maintain a competitive advantage (Traveler, 2019). While managers appear to appreciate the importance of talent management, they often do not manage employees effectively (Collings, 2014). In such case, the need for developing and retaining the best talent becomes the strategic goal for all organisations.

This study aims to identify the factors that influence the intention to implement modern manager's coaching skill that contributes to the improvement in the leadership practice of talent retention and development. Without a focus on talent retention, employees' ability to advance in an organization are limited, and they become at risk of leaving the workgroup, thus increasing attrition and replacement costs for the leadership team (Traveler, 2019).

I have therefore defined my research objective as: "Enhancing the ability of modern managers to implement coaching skills in order to sustain an effective talent retention strategy for private sector enterprises in Malaysia." The research will be framed around the book titled *The Myth of the Coaching Manager*.

1.2 Background of Study

Globally, the current business conditions are experiencing rapid, problematic changes during the Covid-19 pandemic. Despite the pandemic appearing to slow down, most countries are still focusing on the endemic. Moreover, it is becoming increasingly difficult for organizations to maintain their presence in competitive markets due to globalization, stiff competition, and technological advancements, labour shortage, rising cost of raw materials and many more (Aina & Atan, 2020; Free Malaysia Today, 2022). Due to this fact, businesses are shifting their focus from solely focusing on increasing productivity and differentiating themselves from competitors to focusing on their unique asset, which is their employees (human capital) (Ali Almohtaseb et al., 2020). Employees are the most important assets and resources in any organization (Aina & Atan, 2020). The reason for this is that organizations can maximize organizational success if they harness their talent by putting them in the right positions.

During the pandemic period, many organizations have adapted to work-from-home (WFH) arrangements for more than one year, many employees are now reluctantly returning to work. Thus, this trend could result in a wave of "The Great Resignation" that cause many employees left their current job (BusinessToday, 2021). In United States, for example, according to the US Bureau of Labour Statistics showed that 4.4 million resigned under "The Great Resignation" phenomenon (BusinessToday, 2021). Furthermore, a previous study done by tech company Kisi in 2022, they revealed that Dubai (UAE), Hong Kong, Malaysia, Singapore and Montevideo (Uruguay) are the five most overworked cities (Kisi, n.d.). This has resulted a huge number of employees plan to change jobs within a year (Bloomberg, 2022).

According to Demirkaya et al. (2022), the Covid-19 pandemic had made people rethink their career, health and lifestyle priorities.

Moreover, under a comprehensive review by Demirkaya et al. (2022), they found out the reasons of quitting job such as burnout syndrome, toxic organizational culture, the comfort of working from home, insufficient salary, benefits or compensations, relocation, reassessing, priorities in life, seeking for an elusive work-life balance. Furthermore, another survey done by tech company Kisi in the Malaysian context, the findings showed that the top three reasons for employees in Malaysia to leave their current employment are lack of career development (36%), lack of appreciation (27%), and lack of training opportunities (26%). Other factors include pay cuts or not receiving raises in salary, poor management, feeling overworked and a lack of flexibility (BusinessToday, 2021). Additionally, an unresponsive attitude towards new ideas also is one of the reasons that caused Malaysian talent move to the regional peers such as Singapore in search of better opportunities (The Malaysian Reserve, 2020). Thus, organizations in Malaysia should find a way to eliminate such a scenario, "The Great Resignation" and improve the performance of employees to achieve a competitive advantage.

In Malaysia, it was the first time in more than 17 years that Small and Medium Enterprises' gross domestic product grew less than Malaysia's Gross Domestic Product, with -7.3% in 2020 (The Edge, 2021). Among all the businesses, the most concerning was a decline in sales due to consumer buying behaviours shifting from physical to online stores. Due to this transition, especially the small companies have had to deal with the problem of upskilling and reskilling their employee to meet the market demands for technological skills (The Edge, 2021). Due to the over workload or reasons mentioned above, many employees are tired of being micromanaged and told what to do. As a result, they feel trapped in their careers and see little opportunity for growth. Now more than ever, leaders are being called to coach their employees, thereby supporting development, engagement, and trust between themselves and those whom they lead. This is even more demanded during this work-from-home new norm in both Malaysia and the world (AceUp, 2022).

It is common for small and medium-sized Enterprises (SMEs) to have limited resources and capabilities. We acknowledged that every organization (big or small) in the private sector enterprises in Malaysia understands that their managers cannot be relied upon to have every employee of the appropriate behaviour and responses. The traditional order-and-control management approach is not practical in today's challenging and affluent work force (Sherman, 2017). Many organizations are struggling to develop and retain effective employees to stay competitive in this volatile marketplace. There are losing their "talent" to their competitors.

While many Human Resource experts are finding ways and means to overcome this critical challenge. Therefore, working towards a coaching culture wherein managers are expected to work with critical thinking and empower employees' advancement by posing inquiries instead of providing orders is becoming essential. Moreover, coaching is constantly taking place within an organization in order to assist an employee to learn and improve her/his performance, eventually resulting in a more trained, more motivated, more skilled, and more engaged employee by providing them with experiential learning processes from a coach or manager (Lyons & Bandura, 2022). In today's volatile business environment, one-to-one coaching facilitates analyzing and understanding from more instructional forms of training in a flexible and tailored manner. Thus, this new authority style will empower compelling "Talent Retention," of which is also becoming a challenging issue for many organizations to be concern now (Sherman, 2017).

Human Resources experts are aware that the gap is wide between the ideal and the truth. Most managers are either not mindful or reluctant to take up the role of coaching. They favour the conventional management style, of which they feel is easier to apply. Nevertheless, managers are also facing the possible risk of losing capable employees. The present manager needs to discard the idea of "Positional" leadership approach where there is only top-down instruction instead of "Permission" leadership where there are both way communication and trusting working relationship between the leaders and employees. When I began my career with the bank in the early eighties (80's), the order-and-control administration was only the situation, and it is obvious that this management style is only effective in the past (Sherman, 2017).

1.3   Problem Statement

Our business environments are in the rapid, disruptive change, and organizations are realizing that managers can't be expected to have all the answers. The conventional command-and-control leadership is no longer viable in our current workforce (Herminia & Anne, 2019).

As a result, from the above scenario, many companies are moving towards a coaching culture in which they expect their managers to facilitate problem solving and enabling employees' development by asking questions instead giving orders. At the same time, managers need to offer support and guidance without making judgments. This new leadership style will enable effective "Talent Retention" of which is also one of the most challenging problems faced by most companies now.

Though this could be the expectation from many companies' Human Resources specialists, however the gap between the desired outcome and the reality is widening. Many managers are either not aware of the need to coach or they are reluctant to resume the role of coaching. They still prefer the conventional management style, where it is perceived to be easier to do so, nevertheless if they still insist on this conventional management style, they are facing the risks and challenges of losing talented employees.

In today's world, most people do not begin their careers by developing expertise in a technical, functional, or professional domain. In order to do their job well, they had to have the right answers. They eventually rise to people management, where they are required to ensure that their subordinates have those same answers if they could prove themselves that way (Herminia & Anne, 2019).

Therefore, modern day's manager, is no longer to know about what needed to be done, teaching others how to do it, and evaluate their performance. Once upon a time command-and-control was just the name of the game in the past. Now, manager's goal is to direct and develop employees who understood how the business worked and were able to reproduce its previous successes.

Thus, retaining qualified talent is no longer an ideal, but it is required if organizational leaders are going to leverage their qualified talent to maintain a competitive advantage (Northouse, 2016). Modern managers are expected to implement coaching practices into their daily leadership, if not they will continue facing "Talent Retention" crisis and eventually lose out in this highly competitive business environment.

1.4   Research Objectives

The general research objective is to investigate the factors that influencing intention to implement Cent the manager's coaching skill, to sustain effective "Talent Retention Strategy" among private sector enterprises including small and medium-sized enterprises (SMEs) in Malaysia. Thus, the specific aims of this empirical study were highlighted as below:

To examine the relationship between the encouraging factors (e.g., salary, benefits & compensation, work environment, employee engagement, leadership style, training and development) and intention to implement modern manager's coaching skill.

To determine the level of intention of Malaysian general management positions and above from private sector enterprises towards the implementation of coaching skill.

1.5   Research Questions

Based on the objectives, this study attempts to answer the following questions:

Do the encouraging factors (e.g., salary, benefits & compensation, work environment, employee engagement, leadership style, training and development) have a significant influence on intention to implement modern manager's coaching skill?

What is the level of intention of Malaysian general management positions and above from private sector enterprises towards the implementation of coaching skill?

1.6   Rationale of Study

This study focuses on private sector enterprises in various industry in Malaysia. Based on my personal experiences, I have trained and coached managers to chief executive officer (CEO) level in Asian Region in fortune 500 companies, multinational corporation (MNC) and small and medium-sized enterprises (SMEs) in China, Vietnam, Indonesia, Taiwan, Cambodia, Thailand and Malaysia since year 2008. Thus, I have accumulated a lot of real case studies from food and beverage (F&B), hospitals, home furnishing appliances, hotels, financial institutions, and government bodies where these exposures will facilitate my study and research activities.

The rationale of my study is mainly because I always heard from my clients' CEO and the head of human resources that many of their managers are not willing to take up the coaching roles to connect and engage with their direct report. Their managers still prefer the conventional management style, i.e., top-down order, and this management style has resulted employees are not very happy with their direct superior. When the employee turnover is high, it becomes a major obstacle to implementing the "Talent Retention" effectively in most organizations.

In Daniel Goleman's classic study of leadership styles, he revealed that managers who are so used to tackling performance issues by instructing people what to do would feel coaching approach is too "soft". They are uncomfortable as they were so familiar to assert their authority and so they resist coaching and do not even bother to try and came out with excuses of "busy" or "no times" (Daniel, 2000). Thus, I agreed with Daniel's findings as these were the common comments from my learners who attended my Coach Leadership Program.

In one study, 3,761 executives were invited to assess their own coaching skills, twenty-four percent (24%) rated themselves as above average while their colleagues ranked them in the bottom three of the group. This result revealed a mismatch of "If you think you are a good coach, but you are not," the authors of the study wrote, "this data suggests you may be a good deal worse than you imagined." (Herminia & Anne, 2019). Through this case, there is strong evidence to reveal that most managers are disengaged from their employees.

Another example of case in 2016, Mckinsey & Company's study of more than fifty-two thousand (52,000) managers, eighty-six per cent (86%) rated themselves as inspiring and good role models.

But this stands in stark contrast to how employees perceived their leaders in an organization when a 2016 Gallup engagement survey found that eighty two percent (82%) of employees see their leaders as fundamentally uninspiring. In fact, the same survey found that only thirteen percent (13%) of the global workforce is engaged, while twenty-four percent (24%) are actively disengaged (Rasmus & Jacqueline, 2018).

These three (3) important findings consistent with what I witnessed during my training and coaching engagements to develop internal coach for my customers across Asian Region. It is crucial for the CEO and head of human resources to understand the root cause that influence their managers to be a coach.

Coaching is one of the most effective ways to get engaged with people, if this is done effectively, the coach could help their employees to be more positive and motivated with either their performance problem or working relationship issues in the organization.

Coaching with leaders and within organizations is often cited as a highly valuable tool for developing people and businesses. The Institute of Coaching cites that over seventy per cent (70%) of individuals who receive coaching benefited from improved work performance, relationships and more effective communication skills (Carley, 2019).

This study will be useful information to many organizations that have ambition to develop more effective managers to become coaches that can lead their people with more engagement and motivation. When employees are motivated, they will be committed to producing excellent results for their organization, "People Quit People, Not Companies" (Maxwell, 2008).

1.7 Significance of Study

Having diagnosed the research problems and rationale of the study, it is then necessary to mull over the potential contributions of the research. Research is worthwhile when it is of theoretical and practical importance. Against the research objectives, the following subsections discuss the theoretical and practical significance of the present study.

1.7.1 <u>Theoretical Significance</u>

Previous studies have focused on the effective relationship between motivation factors and retention (Ojakaa et al., 2014), what factors influence the coach-coachee relationship to take advantage of coaching in day-to-day management (Chirtina & Grace, 2015), coaching and motivation of human resources (Hajizadeh et al., 2022) as well as the relationship between the role of coach or manager and development of employees (Rahim et al., 2014). However, there is still an unanswered question related to the determinant of factors within the organizational setting to encourage the implementation of coaching. Therefore, this study contributes materially to the body of knowledge concerning the factors (e.g., salary, benefits & compensation, work environment, employee engagement, leadership style, training and development) that influencing intention to implement modern manager's coaching skill among the private company enterprise in Malaysia.

By adopting the Social Cognitive Theory, this study emphasizes the critical factors that influencing a manager or a coach in order to an individuals' actions, which is implementing modern's coaching skill within an organization. Thus, this study can aid scholars to gain valuable experience and develop knowledge and skills and to get the overview of this present study.

1.7.2 **Practical Significance**

Successful completion of this study would redound to the benefit of the private company enterprises in Malaysia. To survive a competitive edge in the industry and most importantly to sustain the profitability of the organization, coaching skill play a pivotal role. Management views coaching as a key component in the implementation of operational strategies and improving talent retention. The focus in this present study is to provide a practical action guide for the organization aimed at understanding the factors influencing the coach or managers in implementation of coaching skills and arranging guidance, stimuli and prompts in ways to assist them to become more engaged in the coaching. Thus, it could enhance the learning opportunities through manager-as-coach. Besides, this study could help the organization to retain the employees within that organization. This is due to not all managers may be successful or interested in implementing the coaching in their organization. Therefore, the organization or human resource management can get some ideas and thought on the possible ways that what factors encourage the coaching implementation in order to achieve their vision.

1.8 Glossary of Key Terms

The following key terms are operationally defined for the purpose of this study:

Coaching refers to a one-to-one learning and development intervention that is collaborative, reflective, goal-oriented and designed to achieve the trainer's desired results (Bozer & Jones, 2018).

Intention to implement refers to the link between a specific direction and an intended behaviour or action, for example, if a situation is encountered, then he or she will perform a goal-oriented response (Hagger & Luszczynska, 2014).

Salary, benefits and compensation refers to all form of pay, rewards, and indirect compensation (e.g., health insurance, organization shares and retirement benefits) going to employee and arising from their employment (Mabaso & Dlamini, 2017).

Work environment refers to surroundings or a working environment where a group of people work together for achieving organization goals and defined as a place where a task is completed (Awan, & Tahir, 2015).

Employee engagement refers to the psychological involvement of an employee in connecting with and commitment to completing their work in an organization (Gatut & Aris, 2020).

Leadership style refers to a process whereby a leader influences a group of individuals to achieve organizational goal productively (Nanjundeswaraswamy & Swamy, 2014).

Training and development refer to a process of improving employees' knowledge and skills that will be used directly in an organization (Gatut & Aris, 2020).

1.9   Organization of Project Research Report

This study concentrates on the relationship between the factors that influence manager's intention to implement coaching skill. This research project is organized in five chapters.

Chapter 1 gives a succinct overview of the research agenda. Against the background of the study, the research issues are explicated. After that, the research objectives, research questions, and rationale of study are stated. The chapter then continues with detailed discussions on the contributions of study, including theoretical and practical significance of this study. In the last section, the glossary of key terms used in this study is furnished.

Chapter 2 contains a comprehensive report of literature relevant to this study and the basis of framework development is delineated.

Chapter 3 focuses on the research methodology applied in this study. The chapter opens with a concise explanation on the philosophical assumptions the researcher holds, which lead to the choice of research methodology and methods. After that, it goes on with details of sampling, ranging from sampling frame to sampling strategies and sample size. After the presentation on measurements, the chapter closes with information on the data analysis method.

Chapter 4 progresses with findings obtained from the statistical analyzes. At the outset, the demographic profiles of samples recruited for the study are reported. In a systematic manner, the statistical tests and results involved in accessing the research model are elucidated. Given the findings, a thorough discussion is provided at the end of the chapter.

Chapter 5 wraps up the study with a conclusion for the study. The chapter starts with a summary of findings in relation to research questions and objectives. Based on the findings, the limitations of the study and future agenda for future studies were discussed. Lastly, the chapter concludes with theoretical and practical implications.

1.10 Chapter Summary

This chapter highlights the importance of coaching skill that used to improve the competitive advantage of an organization. The main purpose of this study is to establish a model explaining the relationships among the factors and intention to implement modern manager's coaching skill. More specifically, there are five factors (e.g., salary, benefits & compensation, work environment, employee engagement, leadership styles, training and development) that influence the manager's decision to implement coaching skill. Besides, the examination of the level of adoption of Malaysian Managers from Private Sector Enterprises towards the implementation of Coaching Skill is a theoretical and practical issue.

Literature Review

2.1 Introduction

This chapter situates the literature relevant to the present study. The first section reviews a string of coaching related research, outlining the importance of coaching and its driving factors. After that, some encouraging factors such as salary, benefits & compensation, work environment, employee engagement, leadership styles, training and development are then discussed that establish the research framework. Finally, the research framework and hypothesis development are highlighted to conclude this chapter.

2.2 Coaching

The term coach originally referred to a vehicle that moved individuals from one place to another (Kim et al., 2013). In general, having a coach in sports was seen as a way of motivating players and improving their performance since the verb coaching originated in sports and the noun coach refers to a trainer or leader (Evered & Selman, 1989). Eventually, other organizations and business managers recognized the value of coaches (Kim et al., 2013). This can be proved that coaching has been associated with improved productivity and increased profits in organizations in practice circles as managers have started coaching their employees to achieve high levels of productivity (de Haan et al., 2011). Thus, there was a general perception of greater effectiveness in the employees who were provided with coaching as well as a higher level of satisfaction among them.

Due to the rapid pace of change and the lack of available managers to mentor or guide, it is often the case that employees require an extensive amount of information and emotional support in many organization (Fey et al., 2022). As this need grows, coaching has become more in demand to achieve business or project success. Coaching is likely a hallmark of organizations that aim to improve skills and performance, support growth opportunities, and address business challenges over time (Latham et al., 2008; London & Smither, 2002). Hence, practitioners within an organization can use such knowledge to select and develop effective managers and leaders and to understand and manage employee attitudes and behaviours.

Furthermore, coaching has been studied actively for at least two decades, and its benefits are mounting. Regardless of the medley of coaching definitions (see Table 2.1), the fundamental core of coaching involves one-to-one systematic interpersonal interactions between a coach and a coachee to promote learning and change (Terblanche, 2022). Several literatures (e.g., Brandes & Lai, 2022; Hamlin et al., 2006; Terblanche, 2022; Wageman, 2001) have delineated that coaching is the idea that leader coaching behaviours can directly affect employees' engagement with their tasks. This is because they can help resolve interpersonal problems that may impede progress and the degree to which employees accept collective responsibility for performance outcomes.

A proliferation of research studies support the view that coaching enhances group processes as well as the level of employee satisfaction (Boyce et al., 2010; London & Smither, 2002; Zhang et al., 2015), ultimately reducing the turnover rate within an organization. For instance, Boyce et al. (2010) studied the effect on the coach-client relationship that the fit between the client and coach influences the coaching program success. They found that coach personal characteristics, managerial and learning styles as well as job-related support could play an important role to influence client-coach relationships in order to significantly impact on project success. Another study done by Hui et al. (2021), they said that coaching may have a different impact on an individual depending on how closely motivational cues implicit in their environment match or fit his/her dispositional beliefs. They also found that coaching is a form of goal-oriented behaviour performed by coach managers to improve performance and adaptation within an organization. Hence, this shed light on the importance of coaching in the development and performance of an organization.

Coaching can play a critical role in influencing employee performance (Azanza et al., 2022; Hui et al., 2021; Pousa et al., 2020). Hence, most organizations intend to allocate adequate financial resources for the purpose of coaching of their workplace. In response to a call from Bozer and Jones (2018), this present study examines what factors are important to influence the intention to implement coaching skill within an organizations among coaches or managers in the Malaysian context. Obtaining a better understanding of the factors that determine the intention to implement coaching will improve and sustain a "Talent Retention Strategy" for private enterprise in Malaysia.

Table 2.1: *The Summary of the Definition of Coaching*

Author (s)/ Year	Definition
Azanza et al. (2022)	Coaching is a systematized, structured, change-oriented learning process, which provides specific tools according to interests. Eventually, it leads to individual and organizational benefits through challenge and support.
Robb et al. (2022)	Coaching is an effective way of encouraging change, enhancing perceptions of a supportive culture of innovation, inspiring goal commitment, and fostering collaborative learning within organizations.
Brandes and Lai (2022)	Coaching is one of the change interventions that draws upon the effectiveness of interpersonal interactions, professional relationships, and employees' strengths to enhance desired yields.
Hui et al. (2021)	Coaching refers to "a component of effective leadership, a goal-oriented developmental practice that guiding and facilitating recipients' achievement of goals for performance improvement and development".
Pousa et al. (2020)	Coaching is defined as "a developmental process initiated by the sales manager, with the goal of helping salespeople and other frontline employees increase their awareness, develop new competences by actively participating in the learning process and eventually achieve higher performance".
Ballesteros-Sánchez et al. (2019)	Coaching refers to "a professional relationship between a coach and a coachee in which the coach, by the use of powerful questions and active listening, addresses issues and challenges and helps the coachee to develop and change mental, behavioural, emotional, and learning patterns. This empowers the coachee to achieve important personal and professional goals".

Milner et al. (2018)	"Coaching is a skillset involving a dialogue between a coach and one or more coachee (those being coached aims to enhance the potential of the coachee".
Grant (2017)	Coaching refers to "the use of coaching methodologies in the workplace for the purpose of helping employees, managers and leaders attain work-related goals in terms of skills, performance or developmental outcomes".
Dahling et al. (2016)	Coaching is a process to improve performance and address personal challenges with subordinates through feedback, behavioural modelling, and goal setting.
Rekalde et al. (2015)	Coaching is "a tool to contribute to and assist in developing strategies that favour managers' personal and professional growth. It provides them with permanent transformative learning in one or more of their visible behaviours and affects the behaviour and performance of their direct collaborators".
Kim et al. (2013)	Coaching is defined as an appropriate managerial and leadership practice that contributes to employee learning and effectiveness through one-to-one conversations, listening and asking questions, as well as providing valuable feedback.
Slåtten et al. (2011)	Coaching is a process for improving present and future performance through a close collaboration between the coach and employee.
Gray et al. (2011)	Coaching is a one-to-one interaction that is experiential, individualized, grounded in mutual trust, and based on data from multiple perspectives. Coaching is designed to enhance an individual's ability to meet short- and long-term goals.

Boyce et al. (2010)	Coaching is a one-on-one helping relationship between a coach and member which is entered into mutual agreement to improve the member's professional performance and personal satisfaction.
Latham et al. (2008)	A coaching includes goal setting, collaborative problem solving, feedback, and an evaluation of end results increased an individual's performance significantly.
Gray (2007)	A coaching process that enables coach managers and leaders to illuminate their organizational vision, a new set of ideas or an experience that acts as a direct learning source and can be enhanced with critical reflection.
Joo (2005)	A coaching emphasizes self-awareness and learning by the one-on-one relationship between the coach and the coachee and to link individual effectiveness with organizational performance.
Edmondson (2003)	Coaching is a direct interaction between trainer-trainees designed to promote and shape desired outcomes, including clarifying and sharing feedback, soliciting input from members, listening to concerns, and being available and open-minded to others' ideas and questions.
Wageman (2001)	Coaching is defined as direct interaction with the team designed to develop and improve team processes, which in turn results in effective performance.
Graham et al. (1994)	Coaching is a process of "creating a climate of communication, mutual respect, ongoing observation and feedback, trust, and a focus on performance objectives".
Evered and Selman (1989)	Coaching is a communication process between coach and member which concentrates on discovering actions that nurture and empower an individual to contribute more fully and productively.

2.2.1 <u>Intention to Implement Modern Manager's Coaching Skill</u>

Basically, the term intention refers to human behaviour resulting from inner motivation (Ajzen, 2011). According to Gollwitzer (1999), intention to implement is a cognitive self-regulatory process intended to oblige goal advancement by bolstering the relationship between goals and actions required to achieve them. Besides, intention to implement modern manager's coaching occurs at different levels of the organization and supports individuals in accomplishing diverse goals. Within an organization, coaching is a strategy that is often used to support leaders or managers during a transition. It also refers to a learning and development strategy that places the employee at the realm of the learning process (Bozer & Jones, 2018). Accordingly, an individual who are high in feedback orientation are more responsive to coaching (London & Smither, 2002). Therefore, managers with an emphasis on coaching can assure the development and growth of employees in order to achieve their goals (Hajizadeh et al., 2022).

Previous research by Cummings et al. (2014), they examined managers' intention to coach employee performance. In their study, they concluded that the willingness of coaching performed by a manager is primarily based on their active engagement. Another study by Shafiq et al. (2013), they found out compensation, training and development and leadership are three key factors that can play an important role to encourage engagement of management team to improve their employee's performance and accountability. According to Joo (2005), he mentioned that learning, development, behavioural change, performance leadership, career success and organizational commitment are the issues related with coaching implementation. Therefore, this study aimed at understanding the factors influencing on intention to implement modern manager's coaching skill.

2.2 Salary, Benefits and Compensation

Salary, benefits, compensation are categorized as direct financial payments (Robianto et al., 2020). According to Mustika et al. (2021), these incentives are most likely of attracting and retaining the key employee. A benefit, for instance, is typically non-cash in nature and intended to aid an individual's well-being. The benefits can be monetary or non-monetary, such as health insurance, paid leave, health programs, pensions, and other company-sponsored activities.

Moreover, Shafiq et al. (2013) indicated that an increase in salary, benefits and compensation is one of proven management practices that can improve productivity, morale, job satisfaction, commitment, adaptability to change, trust, communications, and teamwork. When employees have clear roles, minimal conflict, and opportunities for growth and advancement, they are less likely to quit. Especially for highly valued employees, organizations should train managers in providing clear role expectations, designing organizational processes to minimize role conflict, and communicating career paths (Bryant & Allen, 2013).

2.3 Work Environment

Work environment is defined as the work facilities and infrastructure encircling them when they are performing their duties (Robianto et al., 2020). It includes the workplace, facilities, cleanliness, lighting, tranquillity, as well as interpersonal relationships among employees. According to Razak et al. (2016), for employees to remain productive and to develop high quality lives and work, a healthy working environment is essential. In another study by Serey (2006), the author argues that employees' satisfaction within an organization is influenced by the current work environment. In the workplace, the work environment was associated with pleasant and satisfying work. Consequently, when employees are happy to work in a pleasant and convenient working environment, in turn, productivity increases, burnout decreases, stress and conflict are minimized, and commitment to the work increases (Awan & Tahir, 2015).

Empirical studies have examined the relationship between work environment and job satisfaction, which results in improving performance. For instance, Bakotić and Fiskovića, (2013) discovered that work environment and job satisfaction have a positive relationship. The study also found that employees prefer to work in a risk-free environment. According to Sinha et al. (2010), the development of a sustainable culture in an organization has a significant impact on the motivation of employees. Further, Vischer (2007) demonstrated that a positive work environment leads to a better fit between the workplace and employees, which results in improved behaviour and stress management. Moreover, Awan and Tahir (2015) found that work environment has positive impact on employee's level of productivity within an organizations. In this sense, the work environment plays a crucial role in an organization. In most cases, employees have problems with their working environment. In order to increase productivity, organizations should create a conducive working environment by encouraging managers or management team to provide a coaching.

2.4 Employee Engagement

Engagement of employees is defined as the degree to which the employees are committed to the goals or objectives of the organization (Yuniati et al., 2021). Although there has been a deepening disengagement of employees in the workplace, employee engagement is a key component of a company's success and competitive advantage. Over the past decade, employee engagement has become a popular term in human resource development. However, there is no consensus on how to define engagement in literature. There are a variety of terms being used to describe it, including employee engagement, job engagement, and work engagement (Saks & Gruman, 2014). In addition, employee engagement also overlaps with job satisfaction, organizational commitment, and job involvement but differs from them and has roots in research on job burnout (Saks & Gruman, 2014).

In the past few years, a growing body of literature has suggested that employee engagement is directly related to organizational performance outcomes, such as job performance, employee satisfaction, and financial return (Ladyshewsky & Taplin, 2017). A higher level of work engagement has also been associated with a higher level of organizational commitment (Hakanen et al., 2006). It follows that organizations should make greater efforts to integrate coaching into their managers' skill sets if managerial coaching enhances work engagement, which in turn impacts organizational performance positively.

2.5 Leadership Style

The concept of leadership style is complex, encompassing many definitions and qualities. Based on Berg and Karlsen's (2020) definition, leadership style is a leader's method that involving transformation of strengths into performance capability, which is the key to achieving the desired results. Moreover, Berg and Karlsen (2016) describe it is a process requiring a leader who can handle complex events and be able to lead, coordinate, and influence. Romão et al. (2022) then concluded that leadership style is utilized as an instrument for encouraging, stimulating, and benefiting innovative behaviours in employees.

A leader who actively motivated the team by articulating the rationale for change and inviting others to participate directly, mitigated power discrepancies, and made it easier to learn new ways to work together (Edmondson, 2003). It is important to note that leadership style affects more than just the performance of employees; it can also result in discouragement and hampered the ability of the company to achieve its goals (Romão et al., 2022). Previous study from Edmondson (2003), he mentioned that team leadership consists of motivate input and minimize power differences that can cause the implementation success. Ideally, organizations should develop a coaching culture led by leaders who are capable of bringing methods and tools to the organization to increase job satisfaction (Romão et al., 2022).

A core component of transformational leadership is the ability to coach, which cannot be demonstrated without it (Berg & Karlsen, 2016). A manager who acquires coaching is more likely to focus on goals and relationships and provide more guidance than a manager who does not receive coaching. They also have a higher level of personal development, increased self-efficacy, and a heightened interest in learning (Berg & Karlsen, 2020). As coaching leaders, managers should possess a coaching mindset and have faith in their abilities. It is also possible that they might not be involved in coaching without the ability to coach (Berg & Karlsen, 2016).

2.6 Training and Development

Training and development are fundamentals to increasing skills in the workplace that help to sustain competitive advantage (Ameeq-ul-Ameeq & Hanif, 2013). As a result of training and development, an organization can improve productivity, enhance the quality of work, increase skills, minimize turnover rate, reduce inefficiencies and absenteeism, reduce operating costs, and adopt cutting-edge technologies, human capital management, methods, and products. In order to maximize these benefits, training and development should be tailored to fit the target audience, whether it be an employee or management (Malek et al., 2018).

The effectiveness of training and development can improve employees as well as managers' commitment to the organization (Egan, 2002). Training employees and setting up a learning environment conducive to future learning are required. In addition to clarifying expectations and addressing knowledge assimilation barriers, extensive training can assist employees or managers in achieving organizational goals and increasing their commitment to the organization (Montes et al., 2003). Hence, within an organization, managing effectively requires managers to undergo training and development, indirectly this could encourage them to coach their employees more effectively as well.

Several empirical studies have demonstrated that training and development has a significant impact on organizational commitment, job satisfaction, and turnover intention (e.g., Batt & Valcour, 2003; Choi & Dickson, 2010; Mohamad et al., 2021; Montes et al., 2003; Ridoutt et al., 2002; Seemann et al., 2019; Sousa-Ribeiro et al., 2018). It can seem that training and development is also possible to attribute a lot of influence to managers on employee behaviour. One of the desired outcomes of effective management training is improving management quality. Training and development is the most effective way to help managers develop the necessary skills and knowledge. In terms of training effectiveness, motivation is a critical determinant. To transfer knowledge from the training into the workplace, it takes more than motivation to attend the training (Malek et al., 2018).

An array of subtopics relevant to training and development has been studied in previous research that summarized by Malek et al. (2018), including assessments of various approaches such as specific techniques for training and development, and the importance of quality management training, as well as the critical success factors for quality management. Teamed with effective training, a manager's motivation and capacity to learn have been linked to higher performance levels (Tabassi et al., 2011). According to Tabassi et al. (2011), quality management training is not practiced widely or successfully expect for the manufacturing industry, training is often ineffective. This explains the paucity of research on training and development needs to be considered when optimizing quality management training. It is essential to measure the effect of training and development on the intention to implement coaching in an organization. Generally, managers receive insufficient training for their jobs and this leads to an increase in turnover rate, according to studies on management training. Organizations should focus more on training their managers in light of the connection between management and employee satisfaction and the quality of the workplace environment.

2.7 Underpinning Theory and Research Framework

This study was grounded by the Social Cognitive Theory. According to Bandura (1986), he said that "the Social Cognitive Theory posits that people act on their beliefs about what they can do (self-efficacy), as well as their beliefs about the likely effects of various actions (outcome expectations)". Moreover, drawing from the Social Cognitive Theory, this study holds that expectations about the consequences of manager's behaviour are a strong force guiding them into individuals' actions which is their intention to implement modern's manager coaching skill, in order to retain talent in an organization. According to Compeau and Higgins (1995), they postulated that "individuals are more likely to undertake behaviours they believe will result in valued outcome than those which they do not see as having favorable consequences." In other simple words, managers within an organization who expect positive benefits from coaching would be expected to more highly intention to implement than those who do not expect positive outcome and persist more in their attempts to coach.

To understand the encouraging factors that influence the intention to implement coaching, the research framework was developed and illustrated in Figure 2.1. The research framework proposes the relationship between the independent variables (i.e., salary, benefits and compensation, work environment, employee engagement, leadership style, and training and development) and dependent variable (intention to implement modern manager's coaching skill).

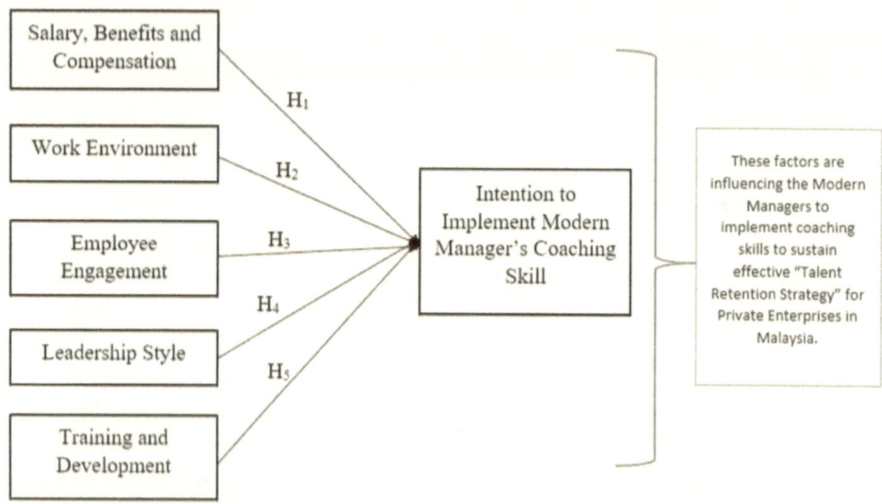

Figure 2.1: *Research Framework*

2.8 Hypotheses Development

As illustrated in Figure 2.1, it shows the hypotheses on the relationships between all variables. In this section, all the hypotheses were discussed and formulated based on the previous literature.

2.8.1 Factors influencing Intention to Implement Modern Manager's Coaching Skill

Coaching has been defined in several ways, for example, it is a process of giving guidance, encouragement and support to the coachee or learner (Robb et al., 2022). Moreover, coaching is characterized as a form of facilitating learning to improve performance and encourage development. However, empirical research on intention to implement coaching is scarce.

The term salary, benefits, and compensation refer to the payments or rewards employees receive because of their employment. These forms of payment could cause the coaching intention. The company strives to control employee turnover, especially when talented employees leave. In the practice of Human Resource Planning, salary, benefits, and compensation are aimed at motivating employees and providing organizational support. The perception of fairness towards rewards or benefits could increase employee satisfaction, resulting in successful achievement of the goal (Mustika et al., 2021).

Furthermore, Awan and Tahir (2015) discovered that work environment has positive impact on employee's level of productivity within an organization. This gave more importance towards the work environment where learning and working is a possible to provide more coaching in an organization. In Shafiq et al. (2013)'s study, they found that salary, benefits and compensation, training and development and leadership are positively correlated to management. They also postulated that the availability of training and development, leadership, and perceived benefits will increase the commitment of managers to their organization. Hakanen et al. (2006) also demonstrated that employee engagement has a positively impact on organizational commitment. Consequently, if managers have high level of commitment, this may encourage them to implement coaching in their organizations.

With previous research evidence, it is therefore proved that salary, benefits and compensation, work environment, employee engagement, leadership style, as well as training and development begin with the leader and coaching could draw this beneficial outcome, in order to retain talent. Managers are taught on how to build "trusting" and "healthy" bonding with their direct reports in their coaching sessions. Therefore, it is plausible that there is a relationship between the encouraging factors (i.e., salary, benefits and compensation, work environment, employee engagement, leadership style, and training and development) have significant influence on intention to implement modern manager's coaching skill among Malaysian general management positions and above from private sector enterprises. Thus, the hypotheses were developed as below:

Hypothesis 1 (H_1): Salary, benefits & compensation has a significant influence on intention to implement modern manager's coaching skill.

Hypothesis 2 (H_2): Work environment has a significant influence on intention to implement modern manager's coaching skill.

Hypothesis 3 (H_3): Employee engagement has a significant influence on intention to implement modern manager's coaching skill.

Hypothesis 4 (H_4): Leadership style has a significant influence on intention to implement modern manager's coaching skill.

Hypothesis 5 (H_5): Training and development has a significant influence on intention to implement modern manager's coaching skill.

2.9 Chapter Summary

This chapter has provided a review of the scholarly materials relevant to the present study. The overarching theory of this study was the Social-Cognitive Theory. Based on sound theoretical foundations, the research framework of the study was developed. It also reviewed the literature on salary, benefits, & compensation, work environment, employee engagement, leadership style, training and development as antecedents as well as intention to implement modern manager' coaching skill as outcome. The following section focuses on the development of the study's framework and hypotheses. The next chapter will cover the methodology of this study.

CHAPTER 03

Research Methodology

3.1   Introduction

To design a solid study, you need more than just a topic, you need a game plan. This chapter breaks down how the research was structured, from deciding on the right sampling method to designing the questionnaire, setting up measurement scales, and testing the process with a pilot run. The goal? To ensure that the data collection and analysis are rock-solid, leaving no room for ambiguity.

3.2   Research Design

There is a kind of discipline to research, a method to the madness of curiosity. It isn't just about gathering data or proving a point—it's about knowing what to ask and how to chase the answer. This study takes a positivist stance, favouring concrete hypotheses and measurable outcomes over ambiguity. Babbie (2015) describes research design as a kind of roadmap, a way of structuring the process so that data collection and analysis don't slip into chaos. Within this world, there are two dominant approaches: quantitative and qualitative (Creswell, 2013). Each with its own logic, its own rules of engagement, shaping the way a study unfolds.

This study leans into a quantitative design because it's the best fit for understanding both direct and indirect relationships between key factors. When working with numbers, two dominant approaches come into play: survey research and experimental research (Creswell, 2013). Here, survey research was chosen because it allows for a systematic way to analyse relationships between different variables. By using standardised methods, researchers can measure, compare, and quantify data with statistical tools, making it easier to extract meaningful insights. On top of that, survey research helps clarify the significance of data, giving a deeper understanding of the research problem. The benefits of this approach are clear, as shown in Table 3.1 (Zikmund, Babin, Carr, & Griffin, 2013).

The study stands on the shoulders of existing literature, anchored in Social Cognitive Theory. It examines how salary, benefits, work environment, employee engagement, leadership style, and training shape the willingness of modern managers in Malaysia's private sector to adopt coaching skills. A large data set was necessary—not just for credibility, but for broader applicability. A quantitative survey method provided the necessary scale and structure, ensuring that the proposed relationships within the research framework weren't just theoretical but statistically grounded.

Since validating and generalizing these relationships requires a broad and reliable data set, a quantitative survey method was the best approach. This method not only ensures a structured and measurable way to collect data but also strengthens the credibility of the findings. By scaling up the data collection process, the study aims to capture a more comprehensive understanding of the factors driving managerial coaching adoption.

Table 3.1: *Advantages of Quantitative Research*

	Advantages of Quantitative Research
1	Tests and validates already constructed theories about how and why phenomena occur.
2	Can generalize research findings when the data are based on random samples of sufficient size.
3	Can generalize research findings when it has been replicated on many different populations and subpopulations.
4	Useful for obtaining data that allow quantitative predictions to be made.
5	The researcher may construct a situation that eliminates the confounding influence of many variables, allowing one to establish more credibly cause-and-effect relationships.
6	Data collection using quantitative methods is relatively quick.
7	Provides precise, quantitative, numerical data.
8	Data analysis is relatively less time consuming using statistical software.
9	The research results are relatively independent of the researcher.
10	It may have higher credibility with people in power.
11	It is useful for studying large numbers of people.

(Source: Zikmund et al., 2013)

3.3 Research Design Planning

3.3.1 Phase 1 - Sampling Design

Clark and Creswell (2015) describe a sample as a smaller group that represents a larger population. Instead of collecting data from every single person, researchers use a sample to keep things manageable while still capturing meaningful insights. There are two main ways to go about this: probability sampling, where everyone in the population has an equal chance of being selected, and non-probability sampling, where selection is based on specific criteria (Clark & Creswell, 2015).

For this study, non-probability sampling was the best choice. The reason? There was no existing list or database that could provide a complete sampling frame of potential respondents (Prayag, 2009). Rather than trying to capture a perfectly random group, the goal here was to test whether the theory held up, not necessarily to generalize findings to an entire population (Sekaran, 2003).

To ensure that the right respondents were included, purposive sampling was used. This method allowed the study to target individuals who fit the profile needed to answer the survey accurately. Instead of reaching out randomly, the questionnaire was distributed online via Microsoft Forms, but only to those who met specific criteria. To qualify, respondents had to be working in a private company or small and medium-sized enterprise (SME) in Malaysia, hold at least a general management position, be responsible for coaching employees to step into leadership roles, and have proven methods for retaining talent. Additionally, they needed to be supervising at least three employees. By focusing on these requirements, the study ensured that the data collected came from professionals who had real-world experience in managerial coaching and talent development.

i) Population

A population, as defined by Zikmund et al. (2013), is a complete set of people, organizations, or institutions that share a common characteristic relevant to a study's purpose. For this research, the target population was clearly identified: top-level executives, such as Chief Executive Officers (CEOs), Chief Operations Officers (COOs), and Chief Marketing Officers (CMOs); middle management, including department heads, directors, chief supervisors, and middle managers; and general management, such as team leaders and supervisors. These individuals were all working in Malaysia's private sector, covering industries like food and beverage, home appliance manufacturing, insurance, financial institutions, and small and medium enterprises (SMEs). According to SME Corporation Malaysia (2022), there are 920,624 entities that fall under this category, making it a significant population to draw insights from.

ii) Sample Size

Different statistical methods require different sample sizes, and choosing the right number of participants is crucial to ensuring reliable results. A larger sample reduces the chance of error and makes the findings more generalizable (Saunders, Lewis, & Thornhill, 2016). But determining the right sample size isn't just about picking a big number—it depends on the complexity of the study, potential missing data, and the accuracy of estimates (Hair et al., 2010).

When estimating unknown parameters, Hair et al. (2009) suggest that any sample size above 200 improves precision. For general research, Roscoe's (1975) rule of thumb recommends a sample size greater than 30 but less than 500. For studies using multiple regression analysis, the required sample should be ten times the number of variables in the model. Since this study involves six explanatory variables—five independent and one dependent—the minimum required sample size should be 60 (6 x 10).

To refine the sample size selection, a *GPower analysis was conducted, which helps determine how many participants are needed to achieve stable estimates (Chin, 1998). This analysis considers three main parameters: the significance level (α), the sample size (N), and the effect size (ES) (Cohen, 1988). GPower is particularly useful for models with multiple predictors (Chin & Newsted, 1999). Since factors like effect size, reliability, and the number of indicators can* influence results, an a priori G*Power analysis was run to ensure the study met the necessary power requirements. For the analysis to be valid, power had to be at least 0.80, with an effect size of at least 0.15 (Hager & Zhang, 2006).

Based on the research framework, an effect size of 0.15 was applied with a 5% margin of error, a power of 80%, and five predictors. G*Power version 3.1.9.4 calculated the statistical power of 92 samples at 0.80 (Faul et al., 2007; Hager & Zhang, 2006). Using a statistical significance level (α) of 0.05, the software reported a power of 0.999, far exceeding the 0.80 threshold and confirming that the sample size was sufficient (Chin, 2001).

While G*Power suggested a minimum of 64 participants at a power of 0.60, Hair et al. (2009) recommended a sample of at least 200. To strike a balance between these recommendations, a middle-ground sample size of 92 was selected as the study's minimum requirement. However, to account for potential errors such as missing values, unclear responses, and non-responses, a total of 300 online questionnaires were distributed to middle management and above in Malaysian private companies via Microsoft Forms. This ensured that even if some responses were incomplete or unusable, the final dataset would still meet the study's statistical needs.

3.3.2 Phase 2 - Questionnaire Design

Surveys are a powerful tool for testing theories, but only if they meet a few essential criteria. According to Colton and Covert (2007), a good survey instrument must be up to date, well-cited, positively reviewed, tested for reliability and validity, aligned with the research questions, and built with appropriate measurement scales. When researchers modify an existing survey to fit their specific study, they need to ensure it remains relevant while adapting it to the study's unique context (Creswell, 2013). With that in mind, this study relied on instruments from previous research, adjusting them as needed to fit the research objectives.

To collect data effectively, a structured questionnaire was developed and distributed online through email, Facebook Messenger, WeChat, and WhatsApp. The survey was conducted in English (refer to Appendices A) and divided into seven sections: salary, benefits, and compensation; work environment; employee engagement; leadership style; training and development; intention to implement modern managerial coaching skills; and respondent profile. Each section was designed to capture specific insights related to the study's core focus areas.

Demographic Questions

Demographic questions played a key role in profiling respondents. These questions covered basic details such as company name, industry, and year of establishment, as well as individual attributes like job position, years of service, age, gender, and education level. One critical question aimed to determine whether respondents had implemented coaching for their employees in the past, providing insight into how widely coaching practices were already in use. Since respondents are more likely to complete surveys that are straightforward and don't take up too much time (Cooper & Schindler, 2008), most of the questions were close-ended with predefined response options. This approach made it easier to categorize responses, process the data efficiently, and ensure consistency in answers.

Measurement Scales for Constructs

To measure key constructs, the study used well-established scales from prior research. A five-point Likert scale was applied across all measurement items, allowing respondents to indicate their level of agreement or disagreement. This scale has been shown to reduce frustration by making responses intuitive and easy to provide (Babakus & Mangold, 1992). Table 3.3 outlines the measurement items used for the six main constructs in the study, ensuring that data collection remained systematic and aligned with the research framework.

Table 3.2: *Measurement Items of this Study*

Key variables	No. of questions	Source
Salary, Benefits & Compensation	4	Holt et al. (2018)
Work Environment	4	Mathew and Gupta (2015)
Employee Engagement	4	Sherman (2017)
Leadership Style	4	Keatlholetswe and Malete (2019)
Training and Development	4	DeMotta et al. (2019)
Intention to Implement	4	van Gelderen et al. (2018)

3.3.3 Phase 3 - Pilot Test

The purpose of pilot test is to detect additional weaknesses in the instrument or research design as well as to ensure selected respondents understand all the questionnaire items (Churchill, 1979). There are several ways of determining the sample size for a pilot test. For instance, Lackey and Wingate (1998) recommended that the sample size for a pilot test should be about 10 per cent of the study population, while Hertzog (2008) recommended 25 to 40 respondents to allow for estimation of reliability and item discrimination. Therefore, this study adopted Hertzog's (2008) approach by selecting 30 respondents for the pilot test.

Before the actual data collection, the pilot test was conducted from 15th to 20th August 2022 (a week). The study questionnaires were distributed via online form to three private companies in Klang Valley, Malaysia through purposive sampling. A total of 30 respondents of managers participated in this stage with a background like the actual study population. A reliability test was conducted on the pilot test responses using the Statistical Package for Social Sciences (SPSS) version 26.0. Table 3.4 shows the general rules on acceptable and unacceptable levels for the Cronbach's Alpha coefficient.

Table 3.3: *Acceptable and Unacceptable Levels of Cronbach's Alpha Coefficient*

Alpha Coefficient	Implied Reliability
below.60	Unacceptable
between.60 and.65	Undesirable
between.65 and.70	Minimally Acceptable
between.70 and.80	Respectable
between.80 and.90	Very Good
above.90	Consider Shortening the Scale

(Source: DeVellis, 2016)

The reliability results of the pilot test data are presented in Table 3.5. Based on the pilot test results, Cronbach's alpha for Salary, Benefits & Compensation and Work Environment were 0.502 and 0.509, respectively. To improve the Cronbach's alpha value (see Appendix B), one item (I think my company needs to change and add something new to its reward system.) was deleted from Salary, Benefits & Compensation. Meanwhile, another item (I am looking for a new work environment with more opportunities for learning and promotion.) was deleted from the Work Environment. Ultimately, the results reveal that all the constructs demonstrated Cronbach's alpha values above 0.70 (DeVellis, 2016; Nunnally & Bernstein,

1994), meaning that the items met the internal consistency criteria. Hence, the pilot test demonstrated that the study questionnaire was ready for data collection.

Table 3.4: *Reliability Test Results of Pilot Test (n = 30)*

Variables	Number of Items	Abbreviation	Cronbach's alpha
Salary, Benefits & Compensation	3	SBC	0.757
Work Environment	3	WE	0.870
Employee Engagement	4	EE	0.930
Leadership Style	4	LS	0.909
Training and Development	4	TD	0.871
Intention to Implement	3	InT	0.912

3.3.4   Phase 4 - Data Collection

This study followed a quantitative approach, applying a mono-method analytical analysis as recommended by Saunders et al. (2016). In mono-method research, only one type of data collection is used, either purely qualitative or purely quantitative (Saunders et al., 2016). Since this study required structured, measurable insights, a survey-based method was the most appropriate choice. Primary data was collected through an online questionnaire, making it a practical solution given the study's time and financial constraints. Surveys are widely used in business and management research because they are cost-effective, easy to administer, and allow for structured comparisons (Munn & Drever, 1990).

Before data collection began, the questionnaire received approval from the supervisor. The questions were written in English and designed to be clear and straightforward, ensuring that respondents could easily understand and answer them. The survey was then distributed through Microsoft Forms, with links sent via email, Facebook Messenger, WeChat, and WhatsApp (see Appendix C for a screenshot example of WhatsApp distribution).

A purposive sampling method was used, meaning respondents were carefully selected based on specific criteria. To qualify, they had to be employed at a private company in Malaysia and hold a supervisory role overseeing at least three employees. Screening questions were included in the survey to ensure that only eligible participants completed the questionnaire.

Data collection took place over nearly a month, running from August 21, 2022, to September 15, 2022. This timeframe provided enough opportunity to reach the targeted respondents while ensuring the process remained efficient and manageable.

3.4 Data Analysis

Data analysis involved both descriptive and inferential statistical tests. Once the survey responses were collected, they were coded and entered into the Statistical Package for Social Sciences (SPSS) Version 26.0 for analysis. SPSS was used to evaluate the measurement model and examine the hypothesized relationships in the research framework. The following sections outline the data analysis procedures followed in this study.

3.4.1 Data Screening and Preparation

Before diving into the actual analysis, the first step was to screen and prepare the data. This involved three key stages: coding, editing, and data entry (Pallant, 2007). Each questionnaire item was assigned a numerical code using SPSS software, allowing for systematic organization and processing. To ensure the data's accuracy and reliability, responses were carefully reviewed for missing values or inconsistencies.

A standard rule was applied when handling missing values. If less than 10% of a particular questionnaire had missing responses, the mean of the variable was used to replace them. However, if more than 10% of the responses were missing, the entire questionnaire was removed from the dataset. Once the data was properly screened, all responses were entered into SPSS. A frequency analysis was then conducted to develop a demographic profile of the respondents, while also serving as a checkpoint to detect any data entry errors. By running frequency distributions, researchers could verify that the data had been entered correctly before proceeding to deeper analysis.

As part of the initial steps, normality and multicollinearity tests were performed to evaluate the dataset. A normality test determines whether the independent and dependent variables follow a normal distribution, which is essential for valid statistical analysis (Hair et al., 2010). Normality was assessed using skewness and kurtosis values, where an ideal range falls between +1 and -1. Additionally, the Kolmogorov-Smirnov test was conducted to confirm the normality of the dataset, requiring a p-value greater than 0.05.

Multicollinearity, which occurs when independent variables are highly correlated, was also examined. When variables are too closely related, it can distort regression results, making it difficult to assess individual effects. SPSS's multiple regression analysis provided collinearity diagnostics, with the Variance Inflation Factor (VIF) serving as the key indicator. If the VIF value exceeded 10, multicollinearity was considered a problem. However, if the VIF values remained between 1 and 10, no multicollinearity issues were detected (Hair et al., 2010). These preliminary tests ensured that the dataset met statistical assumptions before proceeding with further analysis.

3.4.2 <u>Descriptive Analysis</u>

Descriptive analysis is used to summarize the characteristics of a sample or population. As defined by Zikmund et al. (2013), this process helps in understanding the distribution of data by calculating key statistical values such as the mean, standard deviation, minimum value, and maximum value for both independent and dependent variables. These measures provide an overview of how the data is structured and whether there are any significant patterns or anomalies.

3.4.3 <u>Reliability and Validity</u>

Reliability analysis is a key step in ensuring that a measurement scale consistently produces stable and accurate results. One of the most commonly used methods for testing reliability is Cronbach's Alpha, which measures the internal consistency of a scale. This study first applied Cronbach's Alpha during the pilot test phase to assess the reliability of measurement items.

Beyond reliability, validity is equally important in verifying whether a questionnaire accurately measures what it is intended to measure. Content validity and face validity serve as the initial steps in validating a measurement scale. To establish validity in this study, expert feedback was sought from the project supervisor (Churchill, 1979). Based on the supervisor's input, necessary refinements were made to the questionnaire before proceeding with full-scale data collection.

3.4.4 <u>Correlation Analysis</u>

Correlation analysis is used to measure both the strength and direction of the relationship between two variables. These variables must be measured on an interval or ratio scale to ensure meaningful interpretation. The first step in correlation analysis is determining whether the data follows a normal distribution. If the data is abnormally distributed, a Spearman correlation coefficient is applied to evaluate the bivariate relationships between independent, dependent, and mediating variables. Unlike Pearson correlation, which assumes normality, Spearman correlation is better suited for non-normally distributed data. Pearson correlation can inflate Type I errors and reduce statistical power when applied to skewed datasets, making it unsuitable in such cases (Bishara & Hittner, 2012).

3.4.5 Multiple Regression Analysis

Multiple regression analysis is used to determine how much of the variation in a dependent variable can be explained by multiple independent variables. Hair et al. (2010) note that multiple regression is one of the most widely used multivariate techniques in both explanatory and predictive research. This method allows researchers to assess the relative impact of each independent variable while controlling for others. When performing multiple regression, variables are entered into the model based on statistical criteria, with only one variable added at each stage of analysis. This approach ensures that the model remains structured and interpretable, avoiding unnecessary complexity.

3.4.6 Summary of Data Analysis Tools

To meet the research objectives and answer the study's key questions, data was analyzed using the Statistical Package for Social Sciences (SPSS) software version 26. The tools used for data analysis, along with their corresponding research questions and objectives, are summarized in Table 3.6. These statistical methods ensured that the study's findings were both reliable and meaningful, providing a structured approach to interpreting the collected data.

Table 3.5: *Statistical Technique Used for Data Analysis*

Research Question	Research Objective	Statistical Technique
RQ1. Do the encouraging factors (e.g., salary, benefits & compensation, work environment, employee engagement, leadership style, training and development) have a significant influence on intention to implement modern manager's coaching skill?	RO1. To examine the relationship between the encouraging factors (e.g., salary, benefits & compensation, work environment, employee engagement, leadership style, training and development) and intention to implement modern manager's coaching skill.	Multiple linear regression
RQ2. What is the level of intention of Malaysian general management positions and above from private sector enterprises towards the implementation of coaching skill?	RO2. To determine the level of intention of Malaysian general management positions and above from private sector enterprises towards the implementation of coaching skill.	Descriptive analysis

3.5 Chapter Summary

Research is never just about the numbers, though the numbers are what we cling to in the end. It is about decisions, about structure, about the quiet, deliberate choices that determine what will be counted and what will not. This chapter laid it all out—the sampling, the framework, the fine-tuned mechanics of the study. It explained why certain methods were chosen and others left behind, why this group of managers, why these particular variables. It was not happenstance. It never is.

There was a logic to it, a reason for every scale and every question, a justification for why a survey was sent out instead of an experiment conducted in a controlled room. The pilot test ran like a quiet rehearsal before the real performance. The numbers were gathered, screened, checked for their willingness to behave. And now, with the scaffolding in place, we turn to what all of this was leading to—the results. The data, stripped of theory, laid bare. What do the numbers say? What do they refuse to say? The next chapter holds the answers. Or, at the very least, the evidence from which we will try to find them.

Results and Analysis

4.1 Introduction

The main objective of this research was to explore the factors that influence a manager's intention to implement coaching skills as part of a broader strategy to retain talent in Malaysia's private sector, including small and medium enterprises (SMEs). This chapter presents the results of data analysis using the Statistical Package for the Social Sciences (SPSS) software version 26. The discussion covers key aspects such as response rate, descriptive statistics, respondent demographics, and data screening procedures. This is followed by an analysis of reliability, correlation, and multiple regression tests. Finally, the results of the study's hypotheses are presented and summarized.

4.2 Response Rate

The response rate of the study is summarized in Table 4.1. A total of 300 questionnaires were distributed to private sector companies and SMEs in Malaysia that met the inclusion criteria outlined in earlier chapters. Of these, 204 questionnaires were completed and successfully coded for analysis, resulting in a response rate of 68.00%. However, seven questionnaires (2.33%) were excluded due to outliers, while 89 respondents (29.67%) did not return the questionnaire. The number of unreturned responses suggests that some participants may not have had the time to complete the online survey.

Table 4.1: *Response Rate*

	Total	**Per cent (%)**
Distributed questionnaires	300	100.00
Returned questionnaires	211	70.33
No responded questionnaires	89	29.67
Excluded questionnaires	7	2.33
Total coded questionnaires	**204**	**68.00**

4.3   Data Screening

Before diving into the core analysis, the data needed to be cleaned to ensure accuracy and eliminate errors that could distort the findings. This step was essential to remove any entry mistakes, biases, or inconsistencies. The data screening process in this study involved checking for missing values, identifying outliers, testing for normality, and assessing multicollinearity. Each of these steps ensured that the dataset was suitable for further statistical analysis.

4.3.1   Missing Values

A frequency test was performed for each variable to check for any missing responses. Hair et al. (2010) classify missing data as "missing completely at random" (MCAR) if it exceeds ten percent of the dataset. However, to prevent missing values from being an issue, this study required all respondents to complete every question through Microsoft Forms, ensuring that no skipped responses occurred. As a result, there were no missing values, and no questionnaires had to be excluded from the dataset.

4.3.2 <u>Checking for Outliers</u>

Outliers can distort statistical results, especially in regression analysis, by influencing coefficient estimates and skewing overall findings. If researchers fail to review results on a case-by-case basis, outliers may go unnoticed, leading to misleading conclusions (Hair et al., 2010). Pallant (2011) highlights that various statistical techniques are highly sensitive to outliers, making it crucial to examine data visually before conducting major analyses.

To identify multivariate outliers, this study applied the Mahalanobis distance test, which assesses the statistical distance of each data point from the overall distribution. Following the guidelines of Tabachnick and Fidell (2012), the Mahalanobis distance was evaluated using the chi-square (χ^2) distribution, with degrees of freedom equal to the number of independent variables and a probability threshold of $p < 0.001$.

Appendix D presents the identified outliers, showing that seven responses had p-values below 0.001, indicating significant deviation from the dataset. Since these outliers strongly influenced the multiple regression results, they were removed following recommendations from Rousseeuw and Hubert (2011). After excluding these seven cases, the final dataset consisted of 204 valid responses, ensuring the integrity and reliability of the study's statistical analysis.

4.3.3 <u>Assessment of Multivariate Tests</u>

i) Normality

Normality is a key assumption in multivariate analysis, ensuring that data follows a distribution suitable for statistical tests (Tabachnick & Fidell, 2012). Hair et al. (2010) define a normal distribution as the shape of data distribution for a particular metric variable and how closely it aligns with a standard normal curve. To assess normality in this study, graphical methods such as normal Q-Q plots and histograms were used, as shown in Appendix E. When data points cluster along the diagonal line in a Q-Q plot, it indicates normal distribution.

Beyond visual inspection, the Kolmogorov-Smirnov (K-S) and Shapiro-Wilk tests were performed to check whether the latent construct data followed a normal distribution. A normal distribution is typically indicated by a p-value of 0.05 or higher. However, as displayed in Table 4.2, both tests returned p-values below 0.05, signaling that the dataset did not meet normality assumptions. Additionally, all variables in the proposed model had skewness and kurtosis values within ±1.0, reinforcing that the data was non-normally distributed. Given these findings, non-parametric tests were considered for further analysis to accommodate the non-normal data structure (Neideen & Brasel, 2007).

Table 4.2: *Results of Normality Tests*

	Kolmogorov-Smirnov[a]			Shapiro-Wilk			Skewness	Kurtosis
	Statistic	df	Sig.	Statistic	df	Sig.	Statistic	Statistic
Salary, Benefits & Compensation	0.092	204	0.000	0.974	204	0.001	-0.052	-0.015
Work Environment	0.169	204	0.000	0.947	204	0.000	-0.402	-0.037
Employee Engagement	0.192	204	0.000	0.949	204	0.000	-0.437	0.077
Leadership Style	0.180	204	0.000	0.942	204	0.000	-0.391	0.094
Training and Development	0.179	204	0.000	0.948	204	0.000	-0.216	-0.163
Intention to Implement	0.209	204	0.000	0.908	204	0.000	-0.321	0.645
[a]Lilliefors Significance Correction								

ii) Multicollinearity

Multicollinearity occurs when independent variables in a regression model are highly correlated, making it difficult to isolate their individual effects. SPSS multiple regression analysis was used to detect multicollinearity by examining collinearity diagnostics. The key indicators for multicollinearity are the tolerance value and the Variance Inflation Factor (VIF). If the tolerance value falls below 0.10 or the VIF exceeds 10, multicollinearity is present.

As shown in Table 4.3, all constructs in this study had tolerance values well above 0.10, while VIF values ranged between 1 and 10. This confirms that multicollinearity was not an issue among the independent variables, meaning they could be analyzed separately without affecting the accuracy of the regression results. These findings ensure that the study's model maintains statistical integrity and avoids inflated variance issues.

Table 4.3: *Result of Multicollinearity Test*

Variable	Collinearity Statistics	
	Tolerance	VIF
Salary, Benefits & Compensation	0.421	2.374
Work Environment	0.286	3.492
Employee Engagement	0.263	3.803
Leadership Style	0.260	3.844
Training and Development	0.500	2.000
Dependent Variable: Intention to Implement		

4.4 Descriptive Analysis

This section provides an overview of the demographic profile of the respondents, offering a clearer picture of the dataset. It also presents the descriptive analysis of the main study variables, breaking down complex information into an easily digestible format.

4.4.1 <u>Respondent Profile</u>

A total of 204 respondents voluntarily participated in the survey. Table 4.4 summarizes their demographic characteristics, including industry type, job position, years of service, age, gender, and education level. The respondents came from a diverse range of industries. The largest group, 30.40% (62 respondents), worked in manufacturing. This was followed by 25.00% (51 respondents) from wholesale and retail trade, 14.20% (29 respondents) from service-based industries such as transportation, storage, communications, real estate, insurance, and information and communication technology. Another 13.20% (27 respondents) were from professional, administrative, and support services, as well as healthcare. The remaining 17.30% (35 respondents) came from industries such as mining, water and electricity, construction, hotels, food and beverage, finance, and education.

Most of the companies in the study had been in operation for more than five years, accounting for 86.80% (177 respondents). Only 13.20% (27 respondents) were from companies that had been established for less than five years.

When looking at job positions, the majority of respondents, 67.60% (138 respondents), held middle management roles such as managers. General management roles, including supervisors and team leaders, made up 28.40% (58 respondents). A smaller group, 3.90% (8 respondents), held top management positions, including company founders, owners, and Chief Compliance Officers (CCOs).

Regarding tenure in their current company, 38.70% (79 respondents) had been with their organization for 1 to 5 years, while 31.90% (65 respondents) had worked there for more than ten years. Another 27.50% (56 respondents) had been with their company for 6 to 10 years, while a small fraction, 2.00% (4 respondents), had been employed for less than a year.

Age distribution among respondents showed that 41.20% (84 respondents) were between 41 and 50 years old, 31.90% (65 respondents) were between 31 and 40, and 16.70% (34 respondents) were aged 18 to 30. The smallest group, 10.30% (21 respondents), was over 50 years old.

In terms of gender, men represented a slight majority at 54.90% (112 respondents), while women made up 45.10% (92 respondents).

Educational background varied among the participants. Most respondents, 60.30% (123 respondents), held at least a university-level higher degree. Another 25.50% (52 respondents) had completed STPM (Malaysia's pre-university qualification) or held a diploma.

When asked about coaching implementation in their organizations, 69.10% (141 respondents) stated that they had incorporated coaching for their employees, while 30.90% (63 respondents) had not. These findings provide valuable insight into the professional landscape of the respondents and how coaching is being utilized across industries.

Table 4.4: *Demographic Profile of Respondents*

		Frequency	Per cent
Industry (Company)	Services (Transportation & Storage, Communications, Real Estate, Insurance and Information & Communication Technology)	29	14.20
	Other Services (Professional, Administrative & Support Services and Health)	27	13.20
	Industry (Mining, Water and Electricity)	4	2.00
	Manufacturing	62	30.4

	Construction	4	2.00
	Wholesale and Retail	51	25.00
	Hotel	2	1.00
	Food and Beverage	9	4.40
	Finance	14	6.90
	Education	2	1.00
Year of establishment (Company)	Less than five (5) years	27	13.20
	More than five (5) years	177	86.80
Job position	General management	58	28.40
	Middle management	138	67.60
	Top management	8	3.90
Year of service in this current company	Less than one (1) year	4	2.00
	1-5 years	79	38.70
	6-10 years	56	27.50
	More than ten (10) years	65	31.90
Age	18-30	34	16.70
	31-40	65	31.90
	41-50	84	41.20
	51-60	19	9.30
	Aged 60 and above	2	1.00
Gender	Male	112	54.90
	Female	92	45.10
Education level	SPM or lower	25	12.30
	STPM/Diploma	52	25.50
	Degree	106	52.00
	Master	17	8.30
	Others (Professional certificate such as ACCA and Adults learners)	4	2.00

Note: n=204

4.4.2 <u>Descriptive Analysis of Research Constructs</u>

The descriptive analysis focused on statistical measures such as the mean, standard deviation, and variance for each research construct. In this study, salary, benefits and compensation, work environment, employee engagement, leadership style, and training and development were considered independent variables, while the intention to implement modern managerial coaching skills served as the dependent variable. The findings in Table 4.5 indicate that among all constructs, training and development had the highest mean value (3.85), whereas the intention to implement coaching had the lowest mean value (3.32) on a five-point Likert scale. The standard deviations for all constructs were below 1.00, which suggests that the variation in responses was minimal, indicating that respondents shared similar perceptions regarding these constructs (NIH, n.d.). The following sections provide a breakdown of the descriptive statistics for each construct.

Table 4.5: *Descriptive Statistics of Constructs*

Constructs	Minimum	Maximum	Mean	Std. Deviation	Variance
Salary, Benefits & Compensation	1.33	5.00	3.33	0.761	0.580
Work Environment	1.67	5.00	3.62	0.773	0.598
Employee Engagement	1.00	5.00	3.55	0.776	0.602
Leadership Style	1.75	5.00	3.65	0.722	0.521
Training and Development	2.00	5.00	3.85	0.661	0.437
Intention to Implement	1.00	5.00	3.32	0.774	0.600

i) Salary, Benefits and Compensation

Table 4.6 presents the descriptive statistics related to salary, benefits, and compensation. This construct included three items. The highest mean value (3.60) was associated with the statement, "I am satisfied with the existing company's compensation system," indicating a relatively positive perception of current compensation structures. Meanwhile, the lowest mean value (3.06) corresponded to the statement, "I think that the purpose of a single compensation system is good enough to motivate employees," reflecting a more neutral stance on whether a standardized compensation approach is effective in driving employee motivation.

Table 4.6: *Descriptive Statistics of Salary, Benefits and Compensation*

	N	Mean	Std. Deviation
I am satisfied with the existing company's compensation system.	204	3.60	0.803
I think that the salary system of my company good enough to prevent me from searching for another job.	204	3.31	0.931
I think that the purpose of single compensation system good enough to motivate employee.	204	3.06	1.037

ii) Work Environment

The descriptive statistics for the work environment are displayed in Table 4.7. This construct was measured using three items. The highest mean value (3.76) was observed for the statement, "My company provides me with career growth opportunities," suggesting that employees recognized their organization's efforts in facilitating professional advancement. On the other hand, the lowest mean (3.54) was associated with the statement, "I think that my company has a high-quality work environment," indicating slightly less consensus on overall workplace conditions.

Table 4.7: *Descriptive Statistics of Work Environment*

	N	Mean	Std. Deviation
I think that my company having high quality work environment.	204	3.54	0.867
My company provides me with career growth opportunities.	204	3.76	0.862
I am satisfied with the current work environment at my company.	204	3.55	0.927

iii) Employee Engagement

Table 4.8 presents the descriptive statistics for employee engagement, which was measured using four items. The highest mean value (3.63) was assigned to the statement, "My company provides adequate support for employees," reflecting a general agreement that employees felt supported within their work environment. Meanwhile, the lowest mean values (3.50) were shared by the statements, "My company engages employees in career development and planning discussions" and "My company's management provides regular feedback for employees," indicating a relatively lower perception of structured engagement initiatives.

Table 4.8: *Descriptive Statistics of Employee Engagement*

	N	Mean	Std. Deviation
My company provides employee-centred internal programs for enhancing employee engagement.	204	3.55	0.900
My company engages employees in career development and planning discussions.	204	3.50	0.907
My company provides adequate support for employees.	204	3.63	0.818
My company's management provide regular feedback for the employees.	204	3.50	0.879

iv) Leadership Style

Table 4.9 outlines the descriptive statistics for leadership style, which included four items. The highest mean value (3.72) was linked to the statement, "Leaders in my company protect the team when faced with critical situations," suggesting that employees valued their leadership's crisis management capabilities. The lowest mean (3.60) was recorded for the statement, "Company management makes efforts for talent retention as part of the core business strategy," indicating a slightly lower agreement regarding leadership's emphasis on long-term talent retention.

Table 4.9: *Descriptive Statistics of Leadership Style*

	N	Mean	Std. Deviation
Leaders in my company protect the team when faced with critical situations.	204	3.72	0.785
Company's management make efforts for talent retention part of the core business strategy.	204	3.60	0.827
Leaders in my company are flexible in adapting, understanding, and recognizing personal views and needs.	204	3.63	0.898
Leaders in my company provide strategies that impact company performance and employee retention.	204	3.66	0.781

v) Training and Development

The descriptive statistics for training and development are shown in Table 4.10. This construct was measured using four items. The highest mean value (3.87) corresponded to the statement, "My company provides coaching or training to employees for enhancing their skills," suggesting strong recognition of the organization's investment in professional development. The lowest mean (3.68) was linked to the statement, "My company implements effective development and training programs," indicating a slightly lower but still positive perception of training effectiveness.

Table 4.10: *Descriptive Statistics of Training and Development*

	N	Mean	Std. Deviation
My company provides coaching or training to employees for enhancing their skills.	204	3.87	0.802
My company implements effective development and training in my company.	204	3.68	0.844
My company provides the required training and essential skills to employees.	204	3.81	0.726
Training and development have an impact on employee retention.	204	4.03	0.775

vi) Intention to Implement

To address the second research objective, the level of intention to implement modern managerial coaching skills was analyzed using descriptive statistics. Table 4.11 provides the breakdown of this construct, which included three items. The highest mean value (3.38) was recorded for the statement, "I have already planned precisely what I will do as my first step to implementing Modern Manager's Coaching Skill in my company," reflecting a moderate level of planning and commitment. The lowest mean value (3.28) was linked to the statement, "I have already planned precisely where to engage in my first step to implementing Modern Manager's Coaching Skill in my company," indicating slightly less clarity in determining the specific location or context for implementation.

These results provide a detailed view of how respondents perceive various factors related to managerial coaching adoption within their organizations.

Table 4.11: *Descriptive Statistics of Intention to Implement*

	N	Mean	Std. Deviation
I have already planned precisely what I will do as my first step to implementing Modern Manager's Coaching Skill in my company.	204	3.38	0.800
I have already planned precisely when to engage in my first step to implementing Modern Manager's Coaching Skill in my company.	204	3.29	0.814
I have already planned precisely where to engage in my first step to implementing Modern Manager's Coaching Skill in my company.	204	3.28	0.797

4.5 Reliability Test

Reliability in research refers to the stability and consistency of an instrument when measuring a concept (Sekaran & Bougie, 2016). In this study, the reliability of each construct was assessed using Cronbach's alpha, a widely accepted measure of internal consistency. According to Nunnally and Bernstein (1994), a Cronbach's alpha value above 0.70 indicates good reliability. The results, as shown in Table 4.12, confirm strong internal consistency across all constructs: salary, benefits, and compensation (0.756); work environment (0.844); employee engagement (0.907); leadership style (0.898); training and development (0.860); and intention to implement (0.961). These values indicate that the measurement items used for each construct were consistent and reliable (see Appendix F for further details).

Table 4.12: *Reliability of Research Constructs*

Construct	No. of Items	Cronbach's Alpha
Salary, Benefits & Compensation	3	0.756
Work Environment	3	0.844
Employee Engagement	4	0.907
Leadership Style	4	0.898
Training and Development	4	0.860
Intention to Implement	3	0.961

4.6 Correlation Analysis

To understand how the study variables were related, a correlation analysis was conducted. Since the dataset did not follow a normal distribution, Spearman's rank correlation coefficients were used instead of Pearson's correlation (Neideen & Brasel, 2007). The bivariate correlations between the dependent variable (intention to implement) and independent variables (salary, benefits, and compensation; work environment; employee engagement; leadership style; and training and development) are summarized in Table 4.13. The findings indicate significant relationships between these variables. Additionally, the analysis confirmed that multicollinearity was not an issue, as all correlation coefficients (r) were below 0.90. This ensures that the data is suitable for multiple regression analysis (Kira, 2013).

Table 4.13: *Spearman's Rank Correlation Results*

	Salary, Benefits & Compensation	Work Environment	Employee Engagement	Leadership Style	Training and Development	Intention to Implement
Salary, Benefits & Compensation	1					
Work Environment	.711**	1				
Employee Engagement	.663**	.778**	1			
Leadership Style	.661**	.747**	.803**	1		
Training and Development	.467**	.585**	.610**	.650**	1	
Intention to Implement	.195**	.215**	.294**	.349**	.397**	1

** Significant at the 0.01 level (2-tailed).

4.7 Multiple Regression Analysis

With no normality or multicollinearity concerns detected, the next step was to conduct multiple regression analysis. This analysis aimed to determine how the independent variables—salary, benefits, and compensation; work environment; employee engagement; leadership style; and training and development—influenced the dependent variable, intention to implement modern managerial coaching skills. The findings presented in Table 4.14 and illustrated in Figure 4.1 address the study's first research objective.

The results indicate that leadership style ($\beta = 0.28$, $p = 0.030$) had a significant positive effect on the intention to implement modern managerial coaching skills. Training and development ($\beta = 0.47$, $p = 0.000$) also showed a strong positive association with intention to implement, aligning with the findings of Sousa-Ribeiro et al. (2018). However, salary, benefits, and compensation ($\beta = 0.08$, $p = 0.427$), work environment ($\beta = -0.23$, $p = 0.053$), and employee engagement ($\beta = -0.03$, $p = 0.835$) did not significantly impact the intention to implement modern managerial coaching skills.

The five independent variables collectively explained 50% of the variance in the intention to implement modern managerial coaching skills, as indicated by the R^2 value. This suggests a moderate level of explanatory power. However, as Granger and Newbold (1974) pointed out, R^2 alone does not determine whether a regression model is adequate. A low R^2 value can still be valid, while a high R^2 does not necessarily mean a good model fit. The presence of significant relationships in the regression model provides meaningful insights, even if the R^2 value is not exceptionally high.

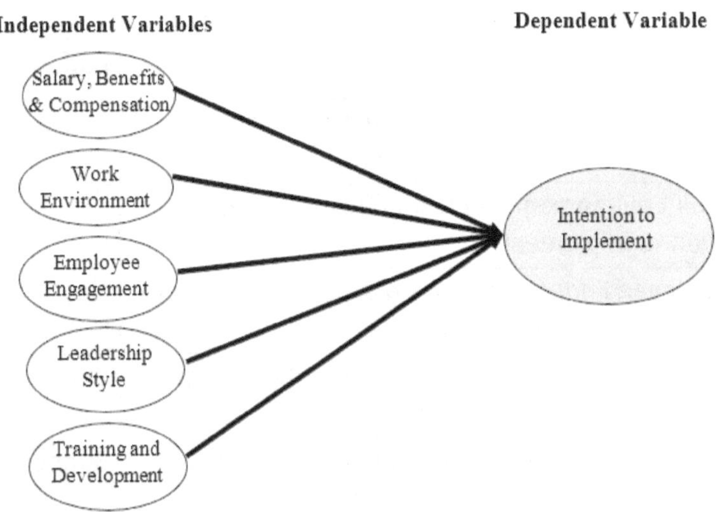

Figure 4.1: *Relationship between Independent Variables and Dependent Variable*

Table 4.14: *Regression Results of Independent Variables with Dependent Variable*

Model	Unstandardized Coefficients		Standardized Coefficients	t	Sig.
	β	Std. Error	Beta		
(Constant)	1.13	.295		3.825	.000
Salary, Benefits & Compensation	.077	.097	.077	.795	.427
Work Environment	-.23	.115	-.23	-1.950	.053
Employee Engagement	-0.25	.120	-0.25	-.208	.835
Leadership Style	.28	.130	.27	2.190	.030
Training and Development	.47	.102	.40	4.572	.000

Notes: R^2=.496; Adjusted R^2=.246; F (5,198) =12.926; p<0.05

Table 4.15: *Hypotheses Testing of Independent Variables with Dependent Variable*

Hypothesis	Result
H_1: Salary, Benefits & Compensation has a significant influence on Intention to Implement.	Not Supported
H_2: Work Environment has a significant influence on Intention to Implement.	Not Supported
H_3: Employee Engagement has a significant influence on Intention to Implement.	Not Supported
H_4: Leadership Style has a significant influence on Intention to Implement.	Supported
H_5: Training and Development has a significant influence on Intention to Implement.	Supported

4.8 Summary of Findings

To achieve the study's objectives, data from 204 respondents were analyzed using a series of statistical tests, including reliability analysis, descriptive analysis, normality tests, correlation analysis, and multiple regression analysis. Every measurement item underwent a reliability check, ensuring consistency in responses. The Cronbach's alpha values for all constructs exceeded 0.70, confirming strong internal reliability (Nunnally & Bernstein, 1994). The descriptive statistics further supported the dataset's validity, with acceptable mean scores and standard deviations across all variables.

The correlation analysis demonstrated that all independent variables—salary, benefits and compensation; work environment; employee engagement; leadership style; and training and development—had significant associations with the intention to implement modern managerial coaching skills. To further validate these relationships, multiple linear regression analysis was conducted. The results revealed that leadership style and training and development had a significant positive influence on the intention to implement modern managerial coaching skills. These findings reinforce the importance of leadership support and professional development in shaping managerial coaching behaviours. The study's key findings are summarized in Table 4.16.

Table 4.16: *Summary of Study's Results*

Research Question	Research Objective	Hypothesis	Result
RQ1. Do the encouraging factors (e.g., salary, benefits & compensation, work environment, employee engagement, leadership style, training and development) has a significant influence on intention to implement modern manager's coaching skill?	RO1. To examine the relationship between the encouraging factors (e.g., salary, benefits & compensation, work environment, employee engagement, leadership style, training and development) and intention to implement modern manager's coaching skill.	H_1: Salary, Benefits & Compensation has a significant influence on Intention to Implement.	**Not Supported**
		H_2: Work Environment has a significant influence on Intention to Implement.	**Not Supported**
		H_3: Employee Engagement has a significant influence on Intention to Implement.	**Not Supported**
		H_4: Leadership Style has a significant influence on Intention to Implement.	**Supported**
		H_5: Training and Development has a significant influence on Intention to Implement.	**Supported**
RQ2. What is the level of intention of Malaysian general management positions and above from private sector enterprises towards the implementation of coaching skill?	RO2. To determine the level of intention of Malaysian general management positions and above from private sector enterprises towards the implementation of coaching skill?	**Not applicable**	As a result, descriptive analysis was used to determine the level of intention to implement modern manager's coaching skill. The result shows only 3.3170 (mean) representing the level of intention to implement from a total of 204 respondents. Additionally, in the five-point Likert scale, 3 represents neutral. This situation means the respondents may not keen to implementing the coaching skill in their company.

4.9 Chapter Summary

The numbers, once raw and indifferent, now take on weight. They suggest something beyond themselves, beyond the neat tables and significance values. There is a moment in every study where the data ceases to be just data and starts whispering the shape of a reality, we suspected but had not yet confirmed. Here, in the quiet precision of regression outputs and correlation coefficients, the message is clear: managers do not coach simply because they are well-paid or because they work in pleasant environments. They coach because they are led by example. They coach because they have been trained to see coaching as an extension of leadership, not an extracurricular obligation.

The study set out to establish the factors that influence a manager's willingness to take on coaching responsibilities, sifting through the expected variables—compensation, engagement, work environment, leadership style, training. The numbers spoke, and their verdict was telling. Out of five hypotheses, only two stood their ground: leadership and training. Everything else—salaries, perks, even engagement—faded into the background. The data exposed a harsh truth: organizations have long miscalculated their investments, pouring resources into monetary incentives while overlooking what truly moves the needle. Coaching is not about financial reward; it is about structure, preparation, and a culture that reinforces development at every level.

The normality tests, correlation matrices, and regression models were more than just statistical exercises; they unraveled the unspoken patterns of management behavior. Companies that assume engagement initiatives will naturally inspire coaching are missing the point. It is not enough to expect managers to pass down wisdom simply because they occupy a leadership position. The study's results make it evident coaching does not emerge from good intentions alone. It emerges from systems that train, reinforce, and demand it. If organizations want managers who develop talent, they must first develop the managers themselves.

For HR specialists, this is not just another dataset. It is a call to rethink how leadership potential is cultivated from within. The findings make a strong case for identifying internal coaches based on factors that predict willingness—training and leadership structures, not just tenure or job title. Investing in these areas is not just about better retention or improved performance metrics; it is about embedding a coaching culture so deeply into the organization that it becomes second nature. A manager who has been taught to coach will coach. A manager who has not will hesitate, no matter how well they are compensated or how comfortable their work environment may be.

And so, the numbers leave us with more than conclusions. They leave us with decisions. What will organizations do with this knowledge? How will these findings translate into practice? That is the question that lingers as the study shifts from raw analysis to real-world implications. The final chapter moves beyond significance values and model summaries. It asks what these findings mean—not just in theory, but in action. What do companies stand to gain? What must they change? And what happens if they don't? The answers lie ahead, in the space where research meets reality.

CHAPTER 05

Conclusion and Discussion

5.1 Introduction

In the final chapter, the findings of this study are discussed and implications are offered for future research. The chapter begins with a discussion of the major findings, followed by limitations and recommendations are made for future study. At the end of the chapter, a concluding remark with implications was discussed.

5.2 Discussion of Major Findings

As organizational change has led to major changes in both tasks and behaviours within an organization, coaching has played a crucial role in maintaining its competitive advantage. Among general management positions and above from private companies and SMEs, this study is essential in understanding the factors that influence their intentions to implement coaching skills, in order to sustain effective "Talent Retention Strategy." Additionally, a research framework comprising five major constructs (i.e., salary, benefits and compensation, work environment, employee engagement, leadership style, training and development, and intention to implement modern manager's coaching skill). The direct and indirect relationships were developed and tested to understand the critical factors influencing intention to implement coaching better.

5.2.1 Factors influencing Intention to Implement Modern Manager's Coaching Skill

The first objective of the present study was to examine the relationship between the encouraging factors (e.g., salary, benefits & compensation, work environment, employee engagement, leadership style, training and development) and intention to implement modern manager's coaching skill by using multiple linear regression analysis.

While the correlation analysis showed positive correlations between the independent variables (salary, benefits and compensation, work environment, employee engagement, leadership style, training and development) and dependent variable (intention to implement modern manager's coaching skill), the multiple regression analysis only supported the effect of leadership style (H_4) and training and development (H_5) on intention to implement modern manager's coaching skills. These findings are consistent with recent evidence that managers who acquire high training application, necessary knowledge, latest skills, informed emotional and cognitive capabilities, positive attitude in leadership and present competencies will have a high tendency to provide coaching in an organization (e.g., Mohamad et al., 2021)

The results revealed that leadership style and training and development are positively and have a direct influence on managers to implement coaching to retain talent, which mean if any company has great leadership culture and effective training and coaching framework, their managers are more willing to be a coach. This finding also in line with the study of Shafiq et al. (2013). Nevertheless, most companies still believe salary, benefits and compensation, work environment and employee engagement would influence their managers to coach of which are their mismatch ideology.

Based on my personal experience, many organizations' managers that I coached and trained in the past decade shared that they understand the impact of coaching on talent retention. However, if they are not aware that i) their superiors understand and recognize each individual's views and needs; ii) their superiors will protect them when critical situations occur; iii) the management is providing strategies and effort into company performance and taking talent retention as part of the core business strategy; they are reluctant to take up the coaching role, as they do not believe their coaching will make a meaningful contribution to retaining talent (London & Smither, 2002).

They even quoted Maxwell's (2008) statement, "People quit people, not companies, " to convince me that their top management must demonstrate effective people leadership. This will increase their confidence that their coaching will enable employees to stay committed to the organization. Besides, they also mentioned that if their companies are not investing in effective training and coaching for all employees, that would provide them with proper training and mentoring to develop their coaching skills. They will not be confident and willing to coach others effectively.

The survey results coincide with what I observed over the past decade. I witnessed managers who were unready to be coaches because their companies lacked a strong leadership culture, as well as ineffective training and coaching frameworks. During one of my Talk Shows, I interviewed a Senior VP from a financial institution, and he said, "Employee retention doesn't begin with resignation". In his statement, he shared that he left his previous company because his formal superior lacked effective leadership traits. In response to his resignation, they countered and offered him an additional

RM 2,000. Due to disappointment that they did not notice his resignation was not about salary, benefits, or compensation, he did not accept the offer. In his four-year tenure, he was frustrated that his contributions were not appreciated. Further, he was not coached by his superior, and he was asked to coach his department's staff. As the working environment deteriorated, his frustration continued to grow. He also mentioned that many key employees followed his footsteps after he left. From the findings of Romão et al. (2022), as they stress, leadership style affects more than just employee performance; it can also result in discouragement and hinder the company's ability to succeed.

Further, he mentioned that many managers in his previous company saw how their talents were lost. As long as the top management exhibited effective leadership qualities, they would be willing to provide training and coaching. As a result, they are more likely to support a coaching culture and eventually minimize the loss of talent. Unfortunately, his formal top management only believed in giving attractive salary packages, providing some engagement sessions to discuss employees' career plans and feedback on job performance, and providing a comfortable working environment that would retain talents. Thus, it may be concluded that these approaches failed to maintain many talents. Besides, their middle managers were encouraged to coach the staff, but the top management team did not coach any managers.

5.2.2   Level of Intention to Implement Modern Manager's Coaching Skill

The second objective of this study to determine the level of intention of Malaysian general management positions and above from private sector enterprises towards the implementation of coaching skill. Coaching is a crucial element concerned with performance improvement of workforces within an organization.

This study aimed to know the level of intention of implement modern manager's coaching skill.

A descriptive statistic was used to determine the level of intention to implement, in order to obtain a more detailed picture of the situation. Overall, a total of 204 respondents were surveyed and the average level of intention to implement was 3.3170 (mean). On the five-point Likert scale, 3 represents neutral. Accordingly, it may be that the respondents are not keen on implementing coaching in their company. It can be concluded that as John Maxwell quoted leaders must do before they want their people to do, in his Law of Modelling (Maxwell, 2008). This company leadership style only instructs their managers to coach but no role model from the top who is coaching managers, they also did not provide proper training and coaching to develop their managers to become an effective coach. Therefore, it is due to this reason that they are not in a high tendency to implement coaching skills in their organization.

5.3   Limitations and Future Studies

Though this study provided useful information in understanding the factors influencing intention to implement modern manager's coaching skill, there are still limitations that could be rectified in future studies. First, the current results may not generalize to all managerial positions in Malaysia since the proportion of general and top management in the sample is likely to be lower than that of middle management. As compared with the larger recruiting force, approximately 68% of respondents in this study were middle management, while approximately 4% were top management positions, and about 28% were in general management. Nevertheless, future studies could expand a similar study to include a broader sample size from different managerial positions across the country in order to improve generalizability and eliminate any anomalies that may have been caused by the small study size.

Future studies can also provide insight into a comparison among these three management groups (i.e., general management, middle management, and top management) by investigating how they perceive the implementation of modern manager's coaching skill.

A second possible limitation is as all participants were volunteers, there is also the possibility of self-selection effects. Most of the applied research involves applying knowledge generated to social concerns, so control groups are rarely created randomly. Some respondents were newly appointed to their positions, which made it impossible to compare their intentions with those who were familiar with coaching. In order to overcome this limitation, it is necessary to conduct another comparison study. This will ensure that there will be a difference between the new manager and the experienced manager regarding the intention to implement coaching.

Lastly, intention to implement of modern manager's coaching skill is influenced by many factors, which are often not analyzed together in a single study. In this study, the encouraging factors of salary, benefits and compensation, work environment, employee engagement, leadership style, training and development are just a few of these factors. Future scholars could investigate additional factors or discouraging factors of managers' intention to implement modern manager's coaching skill, which could facilitate further conceptual refinement and extension. Upcoming researchers could also add moderating variables such as gender, age, and educational background to the present research framework to add to the literature.

5.4 Conclusions and Implications

As a result of this study, scholars and practitioners will be able to derive useful conclusions. A number of theoretical contributions are made in order to highlight how the study of intention implementation coaching contributes to the body of knowledge in this field. Practical contributions refer to the extent to which multiple industry players can benefit simultaneously from the findings. These contributions enable a better understanding of the factors that could influence the intention to implement modern manager coaching skill.

Even though most organizations use coaching to manage their staff, limited studies have been conducted to understand the factors influencing management's intention to implement coaching. Therefore, this study makes several important contributions pertaining to the interrelationships between salary, benefits, compensation, work environment, employee engagement, leadership style, training, and development as well as the intention to implement modern manager's coaching skills from the perception of general management positions and above. By adopting the social cognitive theory, the study examined the perspectives of superiors when it comes to the factors that encourage them to implement a coaching skill. Moreover, this study also discussed the results of the level of intention to implement coaching among the management.

With the current business conditions experiencing rapid change, it is vital that organizations conduct research to understand how this population perceives coaching for coaching purposes. In this regard, findings from this research present significant managerial implications to human resources and the top management within an organization. This study further provides them with the opportunity to make more informed decisions to increase management's intention to implement coaching through an examination of these factors (leadership style, and training and development). As leadership style and training and development influence modern managers' intention to implement coaching skills, human resources or the top management should meet these needs. Moreover, training and development had the most substantial impact on intention to implement compared to other factors. To tap into this, it is essential that human resource management or top management take advantage of it. In order to attain company goals and retain talented employees, they may stress that with training and development they can develop a more effective coaching program that can train a leader so that they can achieve their company's goals.

Overall, it is clear from this study that the research model will assist human resource management or organizations in understanding the factors that influence managers' decision to implement coaching. Moreover, coaching plays a very important role in contributing to the success of an organization. An organization must have a coaching plan with effective strategies for managers to boost performance. To increase managers' intention to coach, organizations also need to focus on other factors besides leadership style, training and development, such as personal traits or characteristics (i.e., gender, income, and educational level) that can effectively balance their professional and personal lives.

References

A.Rahim, N. S., Mansor, N. N. A., & Anvari, R. (2014). Driving the Involvement of Line Managers' Role in Creating Coaching Culture in Malaysia. *Procedia - Social and Behavioural Sciences, 129*(2014), 221–226. https://doi.org/10.1016/j.sbspro.2014.03.670

AceUp. (2022, March 15). *The Importance of a Coaching Approach to Leadership.* https://aceup.com/the-importance-of-a-coaching-approach-to-leadership/

Aina, R. Al, & Atan, T. (2020). The impact of implementing talent management practices on sustainable organizational performance. *Sustainability (Switzerland), 12*(20), 1–21. https://doi.org/10.3390/su12208372

Ajzen, I. (2011). The theory of planned behaviour: Reactions and reflections. *Psychology and Health, 26*(9), 1113–1127. https://doi.org/10.1080/08870446.2011.613995

Ali Almohtaseb, A., A Kareem Shaheen, H., Mohummed Alomari, K., & Yousef Almahameed, M. A. (2020). Impact of Talent Management on Organizational Performance: The Moderating Role of an Effective Performance Management System. *International Journal of Business and Management, 15*(4), 11. https://doi.org/10.5539/ijbm.v15n4p11

Ameeq-ul-Ameeq, & Hanif, F. (2013). Impact of Training on Employee' s Development and Performance in Hotel Industry of Lahore, Pakistan. *Journal of Business Studies Quarterly, 4*(4), 68–83.

Awan, A. G., & Tahir, M. T. (2015). Impact of working environment on employee's productivity: A case study of Banks and Insurance Companies in Pakistan. *European Journal of Business and Management, 7*(1), 329–347. www.iiste.org

Azanza, G., Fernández-Villarán, A., & Goytia, A. (2022). Enhancing Learning in Tourism Education by Combining Learning by Doing and Team Coaching. *Education Sciences, 12*(8), 548. https://doi.org/10.3390/educsci12080548

Babakus, E., & Mangold, W. G. (1992). Adapting the SERVQUAL scale to hospital services: an empirical investigation. *Health Services Research*, *26*(6), 767–786. http://www.ncbi.nlm.nih.gov/pubmed/1737708

Babbie, E. R. (2015). *The practice of social research*. https://www.cengage.com/c/the-practice-of-social-research-14e-babbie/9781305104945

Bakotić, D., & Fiskovića, C. (2013). Relationship between Working Conditions and Job Satisfaction : The Case of Croatian Shipbuilding Company. *International Journal of Business and Social Science*, *4*(2), 206–213.

Ballesteros-Sánchez, L., Ortiz-Marcos, I., & Rodríguez-Rivero, R. (2019). The Impact of Executive Coaching on Project Managers' Personal Competencies. *Project Management Journal*, *50*(3), 306–321. https://doi.org/10.1177/8756972819832191

Bandura, A. (1986). Social foundations of thought and action: A social cognitive theory. In *1986*. NJ: Prentice-Hall.

Batt, R., & Valcour, P. M. (2003). Human resources practices as predictors of work-family outcomes and employee turnover. *Industrial Relations*, *42*(2), 189–220. https://doi.org/10.1111/1468-232X.00287

Berg, M. E., & Karlsen, J. T. (2016). A study of coaching leadership style practice in projects. *Management Research Review*, *39*(9), 1122–1142. https://doi.org/10.1108/MRR-07-2015-0157

Berg, M. E., & Karlsen, J. T. (2020). Coaching leadership style: a learning process. *International Journal of Knowledge and Learning*, *13*(4), 356. https://doi.org/10.1504/ijkl.2020.10033158

Bishara, A. J., & Hittner, J. B. (2012). Testing the significance of a correlation with nonnormal data: Comparison of Pearson, Spearman, transformation, and resampling approaches. *Psychological Methods*, *17*(3), 399–417. https://doi.org/10.1037/a0028087

Bloomberg. (2022, May 25). *How to Deal With Burnout? Best Cities for Work-Life Balance Ranked*. https://www.bloomberg.com/news/articles/2022-05-25/how-to-deal-with-burnout-top-cities-for-work-life-balance-ranked

Boyce, L. A., Jackson, R. J., & Neal, L. J. (2010). Building successful leadership coaching relationships: Examining impact of matching criteria in a leadership coaching program. *Journal of Management Development*, *29*(10), 914–931. https://doi.org/10.1108/02621711011084231

Bozer, G., & Jones, R. J. (2018). Understanding the factors that determine workplace coaching effectiveness: a systematic literature review.

European Journal of Work and Organizational Psychology, 27(3), 342–361. https://doi.org/10.1080/1359432X.2018.1446946

Brandes, B., & Lai, Y. L. (2022). Addressing resistance to change through a micro interpersonal lens: an investigation into the coaching process. *Journal of Organizational Change Management, 35*(3), 666–681. https://doi.org/10.1108/JOCM-07-2021-0214

Bryant, P. C., & Allen, D. G. (2013). Compensation, Benefits and Employee Turnover. *Compensation & Benefits Review, 45*(3), 171–175. https://doi.org/10.1177/0886368713494342

BusinessToday. (2021, December 3). *Is The "Great Resignation" Spreading In Malaysia?* https://www.businesstoday.com.my/2021/12/03/is-the-great-resignation-spreading-in-malaysia/

Carley, S. (2019, March 28). *How Does Coaching Actually Help Leaders?* Forbes. https://www.forbes.com/sites/carleysime/2019/03/28/how-does-coaching-actually-help-leaders/?sh=32a2f07b1645

Chin, W. W. (1998). The partial least squares approach for structural equation modeling. In *Modern methods for business research* (pp. 295–336).

Chin, W. W. (2001). *PLS-Graph User's Guide, Version 3.0.* Houston: C.T. Bauer College of Business, University of Houston.

Chin, W. W., & Newsted, P. R. (1999). Structural Equation Modeling Analysis with Small Samples using Partial Lesst Squares, in Hoyle, R.R. (Ed.). In *Statistical Strategies for Small Sample Research* (pp. 307–341). Statistical Strategies for Small Sample Research, Sage, Thousand Oaks, CA.

Chirtina, T., & Grace, M. (2015). Coachable Moments: Identifying the factors that influence managers to take advantage of them in day-to-day management. *International Journal of Evidence Based Coaching and Mentoring, 13*(1), 1–13.

Choi, Y., & Dickson, D. R. (2010). A case study into the benefits of management training programs: Impacts on hotel employee turnover and satisfaction level. *Journal of Human Resources in Hospitality and Tourism, 9*(1), 103–116. https://doi.org/10.1080/15332840903336499

Churchill, G. A. (1979). A Paradigm for Developing Better Measures of Marketing Constructs. *Journal of Marketing Research, 16*(1), 64. https://doi.org/10.2307/3150876

Clark, V. L. P., & Creswell, J. W. (2015). *Understanding research : a consumer's guide.* Pearson.

Cohen, J. (1988). *Statistical Power Analysis for the Behavioural Sciences Second Edition.*

Collings, D. G. (2014). Toward Mature Talent Management: Beyond Shareholder Value. *Human Resource Development Quarterly, 25*(3), 301–319. https://doi.org/10.1002/HRDQ.21198

Colton, D., & Covert, R. W. (2007). *Designing and constructing instruments for social research and evaluation.* John Wiley & Sons.

Compeau, D. R., & Higgins, C. A. (1995). Application of social cognitive theory to training for computer skills. *Information Systems Research, 6*(2), 118–143. https://doi.org/10.1287/isre.6.2.118

Cooper, D. R., & Schindler, P. S. (2008). *Business Research Methods 12th Edition.* McGraw-Hil Irwin.

Creswell, J. W. (2013). *Research design: Qualitative, quantitative, and mixed methods approaches.* Sage publications.

Cummings, G., Mallidou, A. A., Masaoud, E., Kumbamu, A., Schalm, C., Laschinger, H. K. S., & Estabrooks, C. A. (2014). On becoming a coach: A pilot intervention study with managers in long-term care. *Health Care Management Review, 39*(3), 198–209. https://doi.org/10.1097/HMR.0b013e318294e586

Dahling, J. J., Taylor, S. R., Chau, S. L., & Dwight, S. A. (2016). Does Coaching Matter? A Multilevel Model Linking Managerial Coaching Skill and Frequency to Sales Goal Attainment. *Personnel Psychology, 69*(4), 863–894. https://doi.org/10.1111/peps.12123

Daniel, G. (2000). Leadership That Gets Results. *Harvard Business Review.* https://hbr.org/2000/03/leadership-that-gets-results.

de Haan, E., Culpin, V., & Curd, J. (2011). Executive coaching in practice: What determines helpfulness for clients of coaching? *Personnel Review, 40*(1), 24–44. https://doi.org/10.1108/00483481111095500

Demirkaya, H., Aslan, M., Güngör, H., Durmaz, V., & Rodoplu Şahin, D. (2022). COVID-19 and Quitting Jobs. *Frontiers in Psychology, 13.* https://doi.org/10.3389/fpsyg.2022.916222

DeMotta, H. G., Gonzales, S. J., & Lawson, S. (2019). Exploring Strategic Training Approaches that Lead to The Retention of Talented Employees. *Journal of Organizational Psychology, 19*(3), 48–53. https://doi.org/10.33423/jop.v19i3.2144

DeVellis, R. F. (2016). *Scale development : theory and applications* (4 ed.). SAGE Publications, Inc.

Edmondson, A. C. (2003). Speaking up in the operating room: How team leaders promote learning in interdisciplinary action teams. In *Journal of Management Studies* (Vol. 40, Issue 6, pp. 1419–1452). John Wiley & Sons, Ltd. https://doi.org/10.1111/1467-6486.00386

Egan, T. M. (2002). Organization development: An examination of definitions and dependent variables. *Organization Development Journal, 20*(2), 59–70.

Evered, R. D., & Selman, J. C. (1989). Coaching and the art of management. *Organizational Dynamics, 18*(2), 16–32. https://doi.org/10.1016/0090-2616(89)90040-5

Faul, F., Erdfelder, E., Lang, A. G., & Buchner, A. (2007). G*Power 3: A flexible statistical power analysis program for the social, behavioural, and biomedical sciences. *Behaviour Research Methods, 39*(2), 175–191. https://doi.org/10.3758/BF03193146

Fey, N., Nordbäck, E., Ehrnrooth, M., & Mikkonen, K. (2022). How peer coaching fosters employee proactivity and well-being within a self-managing Finnish digital engineering company. *Organizational Dynamics, 51*(3), 100864. https://doi.org/10.1016/j.orgdyn.2021.100864

Free Malaysia Today. (2022, July 11). *SMEs struggle to tap on demand in post-pandemic rebound.* https://www.freemalaysiatoday.com/category/highlight/2022/07/11/smes-struggle-to-tap-on-post-pandemic-rebound-in-demand/

Gatut, H. T. W., & Aris, W. (2020). The Effect of Training, Employee Engagement, and Coaching on Employee Performance in the Human Capital Division Pt. Bank Danamon Indonesia, Tbk. *International Journal of Innovative Science and Research Technology, 5*(1), 727–736.

Gollwitzer, P. M. (1999). Implementation intentions: Strong effects of simple plans. *American Psychologist, 54*(7), 493–503. https://doi.org/10.1037/0003-066X.54.7.493

Graham, S., Wedman, J. F., & Garvin Kester, B. (1994). Manager Coaching Skills: What Makes a Good Coach? *Performance Improvement Quarterly, 7*(2), 81–94. https://doi.org/10.1111/j.1937-8327.1994.tb00626.x

Granger, C. W. J., & Newbold, P. (1974). Spurious regressions in econometrics. *Journal of Econometrics, 2*(2), 111–120. https://doi.org/10.1016/0304-4076(74)90034-7

Grant, A. M. (2017). The third 'generation' of workplace coaching: creating a culture of quality conversations. *Coaching, 10*(1), 37–53. https://doi.org/10.1080/17521882.2016.1266005

Gray, D. E. (2007). Facilitating management learning: Developing critical reflection through reflective tools. *Management Learning, 38*(5), 495–517. https://doi.org/10.1177/1350507607083204

Gray, D. E., Ekinci, Y., & Goregaokar, H. (2011). Coaching SME managers: Business development or personal therapy? A mixed methods study. *International Journal of Human Resource Management, 22*(4), 863–882. https://doi.org/10.1080/09585192.2011.555129

Hager, W. W. W. W., & Zhang, H. (2006). A Survey of Nonlinear Conjugate Gradient Methods. *Pacific Journal of Optimization, 2*(1), 35–58. http://www.math.ufl.edu/

Hagger, M. S., & Luszczynska, A. (2014). Implementation intention and action planning interventions in health contexts: State of the research and proposals for the way forward. *Applied Psychology: Health and Well-Being, 6*(1), 1–47. https://doi.org/10.1111/aphw.12017

Hair, J. F., Black, W. C., Babin, B. J., & Anderson, R. E. (2010). *Multivariate data analysis (7th Eds)* (I. NJ:Prentice Hall (ed.)).

Hair, J. F., Bush, R. P., & Ortinau, D. J. (2009). Marketing research: In a digital information environment. In *McGraw-Hill*. https://doi.org/10.1111/j.0737-6782.2005.00098.x

Hajizadeh, H., Makvandi, F., & Amirnejad, G. (2022). The effective coaching factors in operational managers of Persian gulf petrochemical company in motivation of human resources. *International Journal of Engineering Business Management, 14*, 1–18. https://doi.org/10.1177/18479790211037222

Hakanen, J. J., Bakker, A. B., & Schaufeli, W. B. (2006). Burnout and work engagement among teachers. *Journal of School Psychology, 43*(6), 495–513. https://doi.org/10.1016/J.JSP.2005.11.001

Hamlin, R. G., Ellinger, A. D., & Beattie, R. S. (2006). Coaching at the heart of managerial effectiveness: A cross-cultural study of managerial behaviours. *Human Resource Development International, 9*(3), 305–331. https://doi.org/10.1080/13678860600893524

Herminia, I., & Anne, S. (2019). The Leader as Coach. *Harvard Business Review*. https://hbr.org/2019/11/the-leader-as-coach.

Hertzog, M. A. (2008). Considerations in determining sample size for pilot studies. *Research in Nursing and Health, 31*(2), 180–191. https://doi.org/10.1002/nur.20247

Holt, S., Hall, A., & Gilley, A. (2018). Essential Components of Leadership Development Programs. *Journal of Managerial Issues, 30*(2), 214–229.

Hui, R. T. yin, Sue-Chan, C., & Wood, R. E. (2021). Performing versus adapting: how leader's coaching style matters in Hong Kong. *International Journal of Human Resource Management*, 32(20), 4163–4189. https://doi.org/10.1080/09585192.2019.1569547

Joo, B. K. B. (2005). Executive Coaching: A Conceptual Framework From an Integrative Review of Practice and Research. *Human Resource Development Review*, 4(4), 462–488. https://doi.org/10.1177/1534484305280866

Keatlholetswe, L., & Malete, L. (2019). Coaching Efficacy, Player Perceptions of Coaches' Leadership Styles, and Team Performance in Premier League Soccer. *Research Quarterly for Exercise and Sport*, 90(1), 71–79. https://doi.org/10.1080/02701367.2018.1563277

Kim, S., Egan, T. M., Kim, W., & Kim, J. (2013). The Impact of Managerial Coaching Behaviour on Employee Work-Related Reactions. *Journal of Business and Psychology*, 28(3), 315–330. https://doi.org/10.1007/s10869-013-9286-9

Kira, A. R. (2013). The evaluation of the factors influence the access to debt financing by Tanzanian SMEs. *European Journal of Business and Management*, 5(7), 1–24.

Kisi. (n.d.). *Work-Life Balance: Best Cities Worldwide in 2022*. Retrieved September 7, 2022, from https://www.getkisi.com/work-life-balance-2022

Lackey, N. R., & Wingate, A. L. (1998). The Pilot Study: One Key to Research Success. In *Advanced Design in Nursing Research* (pp. 375–386). Sage Publications.

Ladyshewsky, R., & Taplin, R. (2017). Employee perceptions of managerial coaching and work engagement using the Measurement Model of Coaching Skills and the Utrecht Work Engagement Scale. *International Journal of Evidence Based Coaching & Mentoring*, 15(2), 25–42.

Latham, G. P., Borgogni, L., & Petitta, L. (2008). Goal setting and performance management in the public sector. *International Public Management Journal*, 11(4), 385–403. https://doi.org/10.1080/10967490802491087

London, M., & Smither, J. W. (2002). Feedback orientation, feedback culture, and the longitudinal performance management process. *Human Resource Management Review*, 12(1), 81–100. https://doi.org/10.1016/S1053-4822(01)00043-2

Lyons, P., & Bandura, R. (2022). Coaching to enhance learning and engagement and reduce turnover. *Journal of Workplace Learning*, 34(3), 295–307. https://doi.org/10.1108/JWL-08-2021-0106

Mabaso, C. M., & Dlamini, B. I. (2017). Impact of Compensation and Benefits on Job Satisfaction. *Research Journal of Business Management, 11*(2), 80–90. https://doi.org/10.3923/rjbm.2017.80.90

Malek, K., Kline, S. F., & DiPietro, R. (2018). The impact of manager training on employee turnover intentions. *Journal of Hospitality and Tourism Insights, 1*(3), 203–219. https://doi.org/10.1108/JHTI-02-2018-0010

Mathew, M., & Gupta, K. (2015). Transformational leadership: Emotional intelligence. *SCMS Journal of Indian Management, 12*(2), 75–98. https://www.ckju.net

Maxwell, J. C. (2008). *Leadership gold : lessons learned from a lifetime of leading*. Thomas Nelson. https://www.perlego.com/book/554815/leadership-gold-pdf

Milner, J., McCarthy, G., & Milner, T. (2018). Training for the coaching leader: how organizations can support managers. *Journal of Management Development, 37*(2), 188–200. https://doi.org/10.1108/JMD-04-2017-0135

Mohamad, N. I., Ismail, A., & Mohamad Nor, A. (2021). Relationship between Managers' Support and Training Application with Motivation to Learn as Mediator. *ETIKONOMI, 20*(1), 119–136. https://doi.org/10.15408/etk.v20i1.15231

Montes, F. J. L., Jover, A. V., & Fernández, L. M. M. (2003). Factors affecting the relationship between total quality management and organizational performance. *International Journal of Quality and Reliability Management, 20*(2), 189–209. https://doi.org/10.1108/02656710310456617

Munn, P., & Drever, E. (1990). *Using questionnaires in small-scale research : a teacher's guide*. Scottish Council for Research in Education, 15 St. John Street, Edinburgh, EH8 8JR, Scotland, United Kingdom. https://eric.ed.gov/?id=ED326488

Mustika, M., Prihanto, Y. J. N., & Winarno, P. M. (2021). The Effects of Compensation and Benefit Satisfaction on Turnover Intention. *Conference Series, 3*(2), 249–265. https://doi.org/10.34306/conferenceseries.v3i2.594

Nanjundeswaraswamy, T. S., & Swamy, D. R. (2014). Leadership styles. *Advances in Management, 7*(2), 57–62. https://www.researchgate.net/publication/272509462_Leadership_styles

Neideen, T., & Brasel, K. (2007). Understanding Statistical Tests. *Journal of Surgical Education, 64*(2), 93–96. https://doi.org/10.1016/j.jsurg.2007.02.001

NIH. (n.d.). *Standard Deviation*. Retrieved September 23, 2022, from https://www.nlm.nih.gov/nichsr/stats_tutorial/section2/mod8_sd.html

Northouse, P. G. (2016). *Leadership: Theory and practice (7th ed.)* (7th ed., Issue 185). CA: Sage. https://doi.org/10.1108/JEA.2008.07446BAA.001

Nunnally, J. C., & Bernstein, I. H. (1994). *Psychometric theory*. McGraw-Hill.

Ojakaa, D., Olango, S., & Jarvis, J. (2014). Factors affecting motivation and retention of primary health care workers in three disparate regions in Kenya. *Human Resources for Health*, *12*(1), 1–13. https://doi.org/10.1186/1478-4491-12-33

Pallant, J. (2011). *SPSS survival manual A step by step guide to data analysis using the SPSS program* (4th Editio). Allen & Unwin, Berkshire.

Pallant, Julie. (2007). *SPSS Survival Manual: A Step by Step Guide to Data Analysis Using SPSS for Windows*. Open University Press Milton Keynes, UK, USA ©2007.

Pousa, C., Liu, Y., & Aman, A. (2020). The effect of managerial coaching on salesperson's relationship behaviours: new evidence from frontline bank employees in China. *International Journal of Bank Marketing*, *38*(6), 1259–1277. https://doi.org/10.1108/IJBM-12-2019-0437

Prayag, G. (2009). Tourists' Evaluations of Destination Image, Satisfaction, and Future Behavioural Intentions—The Case of Mauritius. *Journal of Travel & Tourism Marketing*, *26*(8), 836–853. https://doi.org/10.1080/10548400903358729

Rasmus, H., & Jacqueline, C. (2018). *The Mind of the Leader: How to Lead Yourself, Your People, and Your Organization for Extraordinary Results*. Harvard Business Review Press.

Razak, N. A., Ma'amor, H., & Hassan, N. (2016). Measuring Reliability and Validity Instruments of Work Environment Towards Quality Work Life. *Procedia Economics and Finance*, *37*(2016), 520–528. https://doi.org/10.1016/s2212-5671(16)30160-5

Rekalde, I., Landeta, J., & Albizu, E. (2015). Determining factors in the effectiveness of executive coaching as a management development tool. *Management Decision*, *53*(8), 1677–1697. https://doi.org/10.1108/MD-12-2014-0666

Ridoutt, L., Dutneall, R., Hummel, K., & Smith, C. S. (2002). Factors influencing the implementation of training and learning in the workplace. *Ncver*, 101.

Robb, A., Rohrschneider, M., Booth, A., Carter, P., Walker, R., & Andrews, G. (2022). Enhancing organisational innovation capability – A practice-oriented insight for pharmaceutical companies. *Technovation, 115*(2022), 102461. https://doi.org/10.1016/j.technovation.2022.102461

Robianto, F., Masdupi, E., & Syahrizal. (2020). The Effect of Career Development, Compensation, Work Environment and Job Satisfaction on Work Engagement. *4th Padang International Conference on Education, Economics, Business and Accounting (PICEEBA-2 2019)*, 737–748. https://doi.org/10.2991/aebmr.k.200305.140

Romão, S., Ribeiro, N., Gomes, D. R., & Singh, S. (2022). The Impact of Leaders' Coaching Skills on Employees' Happiness and Turnover Intention. *Administrative Sciences, 12*(3), 84. https://doi.org/10.3390/ADMSCI12030084

Roscoe, J. T. (1975). *Fundamental research statistics for the behavioural sciences* (2nd ed.). Holt, Rinehart and Winston. https://trove.nla.gov.au/work/21136485?q&versionId=44812195

Rousseeuw, P. J., & Hubert, M. (2011). Robust statistics for outlier detection. *Wiley Interdisciplinary Reviews: Data Mining and Knowledge Discovery, 1*(1), 73–79. https://doi.org/10.1002/widm.2

Saks, A. M., & Gruman, J. A. (2014). What Do We Really Know About Employee Engagement? *Human Resource Development Quarterly, 25*(2), 155–182. https://doi.org/10.1002/hrdq.21187

Saunders, M., Lewis, P., & Thornhill, A. (2016). Research Method For Business Students Seventh Edition. In *Pearson Education Limited*.

Seemann, P., Štofkova, Z., & Binasova, V. (2019). *Coaching as a Modern Form of Company Management and Development Tool to Increase the Business Competitiveness*. https://doi.org/10.2991/EMT-19.2019.18

Sekaran, U. (2003). *Research methods for business: A skill building approach*. John Wiley & Sons.

Sekaran, U., & Bougie, R. J. (2016). *RESEARCH METHODS FOR BUSINESS*. Wiley.

Serey, T. T. (2006). Choosing a Robust Quality of Work Life. In *Business Forum* (Vol. 27, Issue 2, pp. 7–10).

Shafiq, M., Zia-ur-Rehman, D. M., & Rashid, M. (2013). Impact of Compensation, Training and Development and Supervisory Support on Organizational Commitment. *Compensation & Benefits Review, 45*(5), 278–285. https://doi.org/10.1177/0886368713515965

Sherman, R. O. (2017). The Leader Coach. In *Nurse Leader* (Vol. 15, Issue 3, pp. 154–155). Academic Press Inc. https://doi.org/10.1016/j.mnl.2017.02.006

Sinha, S., Singh, A. K., Gupta, N., & Dutt, R. (2010). Impact of Work Culture on Motivation and Performance Level of Employees in Private Sector Companies. *Acta Oeconomica Pragensia, 18*(6), 49–67. https://doi.org/10.18267/j.aop.321

Slåtten, T., Svensson, G., & Sværi, S. (2011). Service quality and turnover intentions as perceived by employees: Antecedents and consequences. *Personnel Review, 40*(2), 205–221. https://doi.org/10.1108/00483481111106084

SME Corporation Malaysia. (2022). *Profile of SMEs*. https://smecorp.gov.my/index.php/en/profile-of-smes

Sousa-Ribeiro, M., Sverke, M., Coimbra, J. L., & De Witte, H. (2018). Intentions to Participate in Training Among Older Unemployed People: A Serial Mediator Model. *Journal of Career Development, 45*(3), 268–284. https://doi.org/10.1177/0894845316687669

Tabachnick, B., & Fidell, L. (2012). *Using Multivariate Statistics, 6th Ed*. Pearson.

Tabachnick, B. G., & Fidell, L. S. (2012). Using multivariate statistics (6th ed.). In *New York: Harper and Row*. https://doi.org/10.1037/022267

Tabassi, A. A., Ramli, M., & Abu Bakar, A. H. (2011). Training and Development of Workforces in Construction Industry. *International Journal of Academic Research, 3*(4), 509–516.

Terblanche, N. H. D. (2022). Managers' responses to the initial stages of the Covid-19 pandemic: an executive coaching perspective. *Personnel Review, 51*(5), 1534–1552. https://doi.org/10.1108/PR-07-2020-0540

The Edge. (2021, October 4). *Business coaching: Hope rising from the ashes*. https://www.theedgemarkets.com/article/business-coaching-hope-rising-ashes

The Malaysian Reserve. (2020, January 21). *Malaysia losing out talents due to policies, unresponsive attitude*. https://themalaysianreserve.com/2020/01/21/malaysia-losing-out-talents-due-to-policies-unresponsive-attitude/

Traveler, S. M. (2019). Retention Strategies to Prepare and Maintain Talent for Future Leadership Roles. In *Walden Dissertations and Doctoral Studies*. Walden University.

van Gelderen, M., Kautonen, T., Wincent, J., & Biniari, M. (2018). Implementation intentions in the entrepreneurial process: concept, empirical findings, and research agenda. *Small Business Economics, 51*(4), 923–941. https://doi.org/10.1007/s11187-017-9971-6

Vischer, J. C. (2007). The concept of workplace performance and its value to managers. *California Management Review, 49*(2), 62–79. https://doi.org/10.2307/41166383

Wageman, R. (2001). How Leaders Foster Self-Managing Team Effectiveness: Design Choices Versus Hands-on Coaching. *Organization Science, 12*(5), 559–577. https://doi.org/10.1287/orsc.12.5.559.10094

Yuniati, E., Soetjipto, B. E., Wardoyo, T., Sudarmiatin, S., & Nikmah, F. (2021). Talent management and organizational performance: The mediating role of employee engagement. *Management Science Letters, 11*(9), 2341–2346. https://doi.org/10.5267/j.msl.2021.5.007

Zhang, J., Ahammad, M. F., Tarba, S., Cooper, C. L., Glaister, K. W., & Wang, J. (2015). The effect of leadership style on talent retention during Merger and Acquisition integration: evidence from China. *International Journal of Human Resource Management, 26*(7), 1021–1050. https://doi.org/10.1080/09585192.2014.908316

Zikmund, W. G., Babin, B. J., Carr, J. C., & Griffin, M. (2013). *Business Research Methods* (Michael Roche (ed.); Ninth Edit). Erin Joyner.

Questionnaire

"Enhancing Modern Manager's Coaching Skill to Sustain Effective "Talent Retention Strategy" for Private Sector Enterprises in Malaysia".

Dear respondent,

I am so grateful that you are voluntarily participating in this applied academic research being conducted as part of the requirement of the CeMBA-Commonwealth Master of Business Administration program in Wawasan Open University (WOU). This study aims to investigate the factors that influencing intention to implement modern manager's coaching skill in order to sustain effective "talent retention strategy" for private sector enterprises in Malaysia.

I want to mention that all information collected for this study would be kept strictly confidential, providing no scope for identifying individual responses, as only aggregate responses will be reported in the project report. In addition, the results may only be made available through academic reports and research papers for learning purposes.

I appreciate your time and efforts in completing the enclosed questionnaire, which may take only 10-15 minutes of your time.

Thank you very much for your time and assistance with my MBA research project.

Sincerely,
Gilbert Ng
Email: pb_bert@yahoo.com.sg

Section A: Salary, Benefits & Compensation

Please indicate the extent of your agreement with the following statements. (Please circle O one number 1-5 indicating strongly disagree to strongly agree)

		Strongly Disagree	Somehow Disagree	Neutral	Somehow Agree	Strongly Agree
1	I am satisfied with the existing company's compensation system.	1	2	3	4	5
2	I think my company needs to change and add something new to its reward system.	1	2	3	4	5
3	I think that the salary system of my company good enough to prevent me from searching for another job.	1	2	3	4	5

		Strongly Disagree	Somehow Disagree	Neutral	Somehow Agree	Strongly Agree
4	I think that the purpose of single compensation system good enough to motivate employee.	1	2	3	4	5

Section B: Work Environment

Please indicate the extent of your agreement with the following statements. (Please circle O one number 1-5 indicating strongly disagree to strongly agree)

		Strongly Disagree	Somehow Disagree	Neutral	Somehow Agree	Strongly Agree
1	I think that my company having high quality work environment.	1	2	3	4	5
2	My company provides me with career growth opportunities.	1	2	3	4	5
3	I am looking for a new work environment with more opportunities for learning and promotion.	1	2	3	4	5
4	I am satisfied with the current work environment at my company.	1	2	3	4	5

Section C: Employee Engagement

Please indicate the extent of your agreement with the following statements. (Please circle O one number 1-5 indicating strongly disagree to strongly agree)

		Strongly Disagree	Disagree	Neutral	Agree	Strongly Agree
1	My company provides employee-centred internal programs for enhancing employee engagement.	1	2	3	4	5
2	My company engages employees in career development and planning discussions.	1	2	3	4	5
3	My company provides adequate support for employees.	1	2	3	4	5
4	My company's management provide regular feedback for the employees.	1	2	3	4	5

Section D: Leadership Style

Please indicate the extent of your agreement with the following statements. (Please circle O one number 1-5 indicating strongly disagree to strongly agree)

		Strongly Disagree	Disagree	Neutral	Agree	Strongly Agree
1	Leaders in my company protect the team when faced with critical situations.	1	2	3	4	5
2	Company's management make efforts for talent retention part of the core business strategy.	1	2	3	4	5
3	Leaders in my company are flexible in adapting, understanding, and recognizing personal views and needs.	1	2	3	4	5
4	Leaders in my company provide strategies that impact company performance and employee retention.	1	2	3	4	5

Section E: Training and Development

Please indicate the extent of your agreement with the following statements. (Please circle O one number 1-5 indicating strongly disagree to strongly agree)

		Strongly Disagree	Disagree	Neutral	Agree	Strongly Agree
1	My company provide coaching or training to employees for enhancing their skills.	1	2	3	4	5
2	My company implements effective development and training in my company.	1	2	3	4	5
3	My company provides the required training and essential skills to employees.	1	2	3	4	5
4	Training and development have an impact on employee retention.	1	2	3	4	5

Section F: Intention to Implement Modern Manager's Coaching Skill

Please indicate the extent of your agreement with the following statements. (Please circle O one number 1-5 indicating strongly disagree to strongly agree)

		Strongly Disagree	Disagree	Neutral	Agree	Strongly Agree
1	I have already planned precisely *what* I will do as my first step to implementing Modern Manager's Coaching Skill in my company.	1	2	3	4	5

2	I have already planned precisely *when* to engage in my first step to implementing Modern Manager's Coaching Skill in my company.	1	2	3	4	5
3	I have already planned precisely *where* to engage in my first step to implementing Modern Manager's Coaching Skill in my company.	1	2	3	4	5

Section G: Respondent Profile

Please state or circle ₁ the appropriate answer for each question.

1. Company name: ________________________________
2. Industry (e.g., construction, IT service, banking etc.): ______________________________
3. Year of establishment: 1. Less than 5 years 2. More than 5 years
4. Job position: ________________________________
5. Year of service in this current company: ________________
6. Have you implemented coaching for your employees before?
   1. Yes   2. No
7. Age: ________________________________
8. Gender: 1. Male   2. Female
9. Education level: 1. SPM or lower 2. STPM/Diploma
   3. Degree   4. Master   5. Phd   6. Others (Please state:________)

-End of questionnaire-

Thank you for your time and cooperation

Result of Pilot Test

Variable: Salary, Benefits & Compensation

Reliability Statistics		
Cronbach's Alpha	Cronbach's Alpha Based on Standardized Items	N of Items
.502	.486	4

Item-Total Statistics					
	Scale Mean if Item Deleted	Scale Variance if Item Deleted	Corrected Item-Total Correlation	Squared Multiple Correlation	Cronbach's Alpha if Item Deleted
I am satisfied with the existing company's compensation system.	10.10	2.714	.526	.408	.215
I think my company needs to change and add something new to its reward system.	9.60	4.731	-.165	.098	.757

Item-Total Statistics					
	Scale Mean if Item Deleted	Scale Variance if Item Deleted	Corrected Item-Total Correlation	Squared Multiple Correlation	Cronbach's Alpha if Item Deleted
I think that the salary system of my company good enough to prevent me from searching for another job.	10.27	2.478	.565	.582	.152
I think that the purpose of single compensation system good enough to motivate employee.	10.73	2.685	.391	.365	.330

Variable: Work Environment

Reliability Statistics		
Cronbach's Alpha	Cronbach's Alpha Based on Standardized Items	N of Items
.509	.553	4

Item-Total Statistics					
	Scale Mean if Item Deleted	Scale Variance if Item Deleted	Corrected Item-Total Correlation	Squared Multiple Correlation	Cronbach's Alpha if Item Deleted
I think that my company having high quality work environment.	10.70	3.528	.590	.644	.141

Item-Total Statistics					
	Scale Mean if Item Deleted	Scale Variance if Item Deleted	Corrected Item-Total Correlation	Squared Multiple Correlation	Cronbach's Alpha if Item Deleted
My company provides me with career growth opportunities.	10.47	3.499	.672	.549	.076
I am looking for a new work environment with more opportunities for learning and promotion.	**10.67**	**7.126**	**-.246**	**.135**	**.870**
I am satisfied with the current work environment at my company.	10.77	3.978	.517	.584	.241

Variable: Employee Engagement

Reliability Statistics		
Cronbach's Alpha	Cronbach's Alpha Based on Standardized Items	N of Items
.930	.931	4

Item-Total Statistics					
	Scale Mean if Item Deleted	Scale Variance if Item Deleted	Corrected Item-Total Correlation	Squared Multiple Correlation	Cronbach's Alpha if Item Deleted
My company provides employee-centred internal programs for enhancing employee engagement.	10.90	6.231	.882	.778	.897
My company engages employees in career development and planning discussions.	10.83	7.592	.798	.650	.921
My company provides adequate support for employees.	10.73	7.375	.827	.703	.912
My company's management provide regular feedback for the employees.	10.83	7.178	.856	.733	.902

Variable: Leadership Style

Reliability Statistics		
Cronbach's Alpha	Cronbach's Alpha Based on Standardized Items	N of Items
.909	.912	4

Item-Total Statistics					
	Scale Mean if Item Deleted	Scale Variance if Item Deleted	Corrected Item-Total Correlation	Squared Multiple Correlation	Cronbach's Alpha if Item Deleted
Leaders in my company protect the team when faced with critical situations.	11.03	4.792	.750	.598	.901
Company's management make efforts for talent retention part of the core business strategy.	10.93	5.237	.804	.654	.882
Leaders in my company are flexible in adapting, understanding, and recognizing personal views and needs.	11.03	4.792	.803	.714	.879
Leaders in my company provide strategies that impact company performance and employee retention.	11.00	4.897	.835	.734	.868

Variable: Training and Development

Reliability Statistics		
Cronbach's Alpha	Cronbach's Alpha Based on Standardized Items	N of Items
.871	.869	4

Item-Total Statistics					
	Scale Mean if Item Deleted	Scale Variance if Item Deleted	Corrected Item-Total Correlation	Squared Multiple Correlation	Cronbach's Alpha if Item Deleted
My company provide coaching or training to employees for enhancing their skills.	11.73	4.616	.796	.687	.808
My company implements effective development and training in my company.	11.90	4.438	.850	.795	.782
My company provides the required training and essential skills to employees.	11.67	5.402	.835	.824	.800
Training and development have an impact on employee retention.	11.30	6.700	.474	.312	.919

Variable: Intention to Implement

Reliability Statistics		
Cronbach's Alpha	Cronbach's Alpha Based on Standardized Items	N of Items
.912	.913	3

Item-Total Statistics					
	Scale Mean if Item Deleted	Scale Variance if Item Deleted	Corrected Item-Total Correlation	Squared Multiple Correlation	Cronbach's Alpha if Item Deleted
I have already planned precisely what I will do as my first step to implementing Modern Manager's Coaching Skill in my company.	6.60	1.214	.734	.548	.947
I have already planned precisely when to engage in my first step to implementing Modern Manager's Coaching Skill in my company.	6.80	1.131	.890	.835	.821
I have already planned precisely where to engage in my first step to implementing Modern Manager's Coaching Skill in my company.	6.87	1.085	.855	.815	.847

Example of a Screenshot of WhatsApp

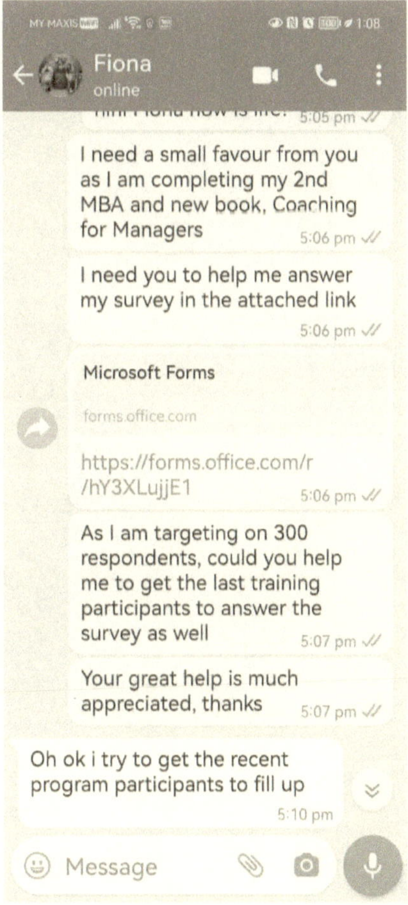

Outliers and Multiple Regression Assumption Test Results

Mahalanobis Distance

Observation no.	Mahalanobis distance	P	Outlier	Observation no.	Mahalanobis distance	P	Outlier
55	32.97236	.00000	1	57	3.84879	.27826	0
1	32.37688	.00000	1	166	3.67951	.29822	0
46	25.67935	.00001	1	112	3.67582	.29866	0
22	23.01455	.00004	1	2	3.66520	.29996	0
47	21.10202	.00010	1	8	3.66170	.30039	0
66	19.18235	.00025	1	199	3.65565	.30113	0
61	17.49696	.00056	1	34	3.62400	.30503	0
59	14.91048	.00189	0	125	3.59153	.30908	0
40	14.53403	.00226	0	63	3.57969	.31057	0
99	13.52745	.00362	0	158	3.53395	.31638	0
27	12.78816	.00512	0	168	3.52706	.31727	0
106	11.54411	.00912	0	71	3.50504	.32011	0
126	11.41682	.00967	0	18	3.47720	.32373	0
33	10.85871	.01251	0	114	3.41990	.33130	0

Observation no.	Mahalanobis distance	P	Outlier	Observation no.	Mahalanobis distance	P	Outlier
151	10.60693	.01405	0	163	3.40201	.33370	0
56	10.56265	.01434	0	32	3.34109	.34197	0
26	10.09331	.01779	0	11	3.32156	.34465	0
49	10.02953	.01832	0	148	3.23715	.35649	0
149	9.78704	.02047	0	131	3.09892	.37662	0
44	9.77081	.02062	0	97	3.01871	.38875	0
45	9.52004	.02312	0	173	2.88687	.40940	0
88	9.19178	.02685	0	191	2.74838	.43207	0
183	9.16777	.02714	0	182	2.73798	.43381	0
62	9.13131	.02760	0	189	2.71357	.43793	0
127	8.97672	.02960	0	170	2.69354	.44133	0
116	8.85354	.03130	0	117	2.69081	.44179	0
98	8.82426	.03172	0	23	2.53503	.46899	0
73	8.79609	.03213	0	121	2.43369	.48739	0
78	8.78134	.03234	0	179	2.42679	.48867	0
115	8.71764	.03329	0	12	2.41398	.49104	0
75	8.63852	.03450	0	133	2.41300	.49122	0
147	8.63529	.03455	0	107	2.39003	.49549	0
200	8.60433	.03504	0	143	2.25330	.52153	0
16	8.59464	.03520	0	174	2.19833	.53228	0
111	8.32389	.03977	0	50	2.18742	.53443	0
132	8.31019	.04002	0	70	2.17061	.53776	0
48	8.14925	.04303	0	54	2.15113	.54164	0
205	7.79781	.05038	0	130	2.15017	.54183	0
96	7.71428	.05230	0	82	2.13884	.54410	0
145	7.70525	.05251	0	91	2.08946	.55405	0
128	7.41928	.05967	0	155	2.08931	.55408	0

Observation no.	Mahalanobis distance	P	Outlier	Observation no.	Mahalanobis distance	P	Outlier
134	7.28976	.06321	0	154	2.05810	.56044	0
100	7.18710	.06617	0	79	2.05665	.56073	0
159	7.04787	.07039	0	123	2.05665	.56073	0
42	6.95228	.07343	0	110	1.82773	.60892	0
144	6.78521	.07907	0	176	1.81508	.61166	0
172	6.78402	.07911	0	187	1.77067	.62134	0
89	6.77052	.07958	0	4	1.73525	.62913	0
122	6.76426	.07980	0	142	1.72586	.63120	0
10	6.63759	.08439	0	69	1.71106	.63448	0
178	6.55465	.08753	0	72	1.69447	.63816	0
153	6.30230	.09779	0	93	1.69051	.63905	0
108	6.25054	.10004	0	80	1.66125	.64558	0
39	6.18112	.10312	0	76	1.58726	.66228	0
17	6.16309	.10394	0	177	1.58726	.66228	0
24	6.06623	.10843	0	68	1.56997	.66622	0
21	5.98461	.11236	0	113	1.44613	.69476	0
13	5.98061	.11256	0	211	1.39720	.70619	0
192	5.94129	.11450	0	198	1.36789	.71308	0
64	5.93668	.11473	0	105	1.34064	.71951	0
186	5.91025	.11606	0	28	1.33387	.72111	0
204	5.91025	.11606	0	6	1.29170	.73110	0
207	5.91025	.11606	0	38	1.21954	.74832	0
209	5.91025	.11606	0	140	1.19978	.75306	0
160	5.88197	.11750	0	101	1.18141	.75747	0
102	5.87843	.11768	0	152	1.15522	.76376	0
41	5.85934	.11866	0	193	1.15277	.76435	0
74	5.84632	.11933	0	25	1.15215	.76450	0

Observation no.	Mahalanobis distance	P	Outlier	Observation no.	Mahalanobis distance	P	Outlier
104	5.79733	.12190	0	180	1.13960	.76752	0
119	5.74249	.12483	0	169	1.12624	.77074	0
87	5.65387	.12972	0	65	1.09226	.77894	0
92	5.63824	.13060	0	20	1.09056	.77935	0
135	5.60206	.13266	0	14	1.08978	.77954	0
37	5.53748	.13641	0	3	1.06015	.78670	0
58	5.53748	.13641	0	124	1.04115	.79130	0
120	5.53748	.13641	0	95	.99627	.80216	0
156	5.53748	.13641	0	109	.94281	.81509	0
157	5.53748	.13641	0	175	.93582	.81678	0
164	5.53748	.13641	0	7	.91383	.82209	0
19	5.47943	.13987	0	51	.91383	.82209	0
5	5.47520	.14013	0	137	.91383	.82209	0
208	5.39378	.14513	0	171	.91383	.82209	0
83	5.35807	.14738	0	184	.91383	.82209	0
52	5.34605	.14814	0	185	.91383	.82209	0
136	5.27297	.15287	0	201	.91383	.82209	0
90	5.13765	.16199	0	202	.91383	.82209	0
150	5.02841	.16973	0	203	.91383	.82209	0
9	4.97203	.17386	0	206	.91383	.82209	0
181	4.91701	.17798	0	210	.91383	.82209	0
35	4.62974	.20101	0	29	.85759	.83565	0
139	4.60033	.20351	0	161	.72173	.86808	0
118	4.43890	.21781	0	15	.63560	.88824	0
43	4.40271	.22113	0	36	.63560	.88824	0
94	4.40258	.22115	0	77	.63560	.88824	0
162	4.35745	.22536	0	167	.63560	.88824	0

Observation no.	Mahalanobis distance	P	Outlier	Observation no.	Mahalanobis distance	P	Outlier
81	4.34005	.22701	0	60	.58357	.90018	0
103	4.30846	.23002	0	31	.44069	.93171	0
53	4.18662	.24201	0	86	.40808	.93857	0
84	4.18378	.24229	0	129	.40808	.93857	0
30	4.12690	.24808	0	138	.40808	.93857	0
188	4.06859	.25415	0	190	.40808	.93857	0
146	4.02848	.25841	0	194	.40808	.93857	0
141	4.00592	.26083	0	195	.40808	.93857	0
67	4.00383	.26105	0	196	.40808	.93857	0
165	3.99210	.26232	0	197	.40808	.93857	0
85	3.94949	.26697	0				

Note: $p < 0.001$, then consider as outlier.

Histogram, Normal Q-Q Plot

Variable: Salary, Benefits & Compensation

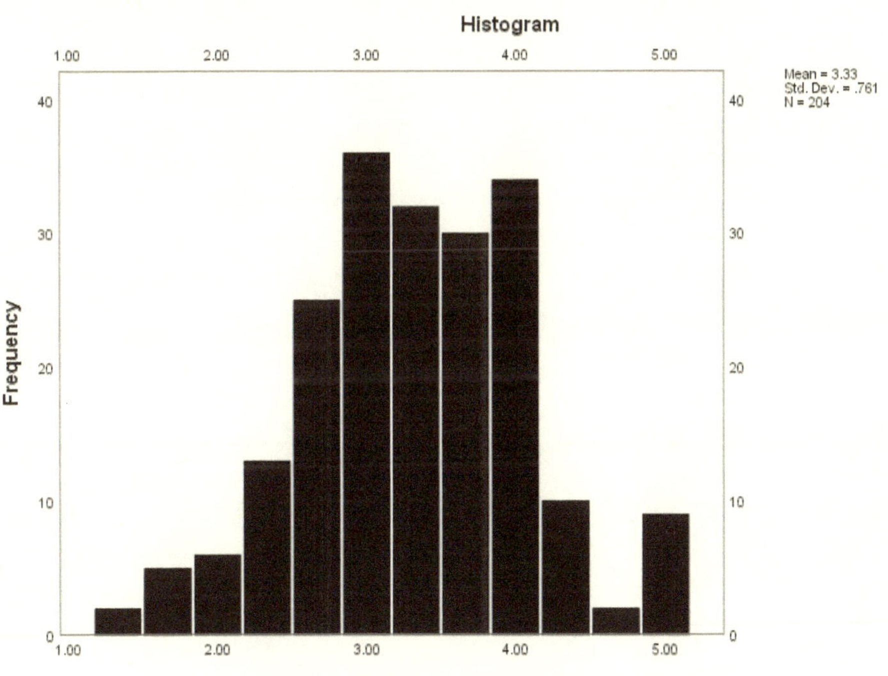

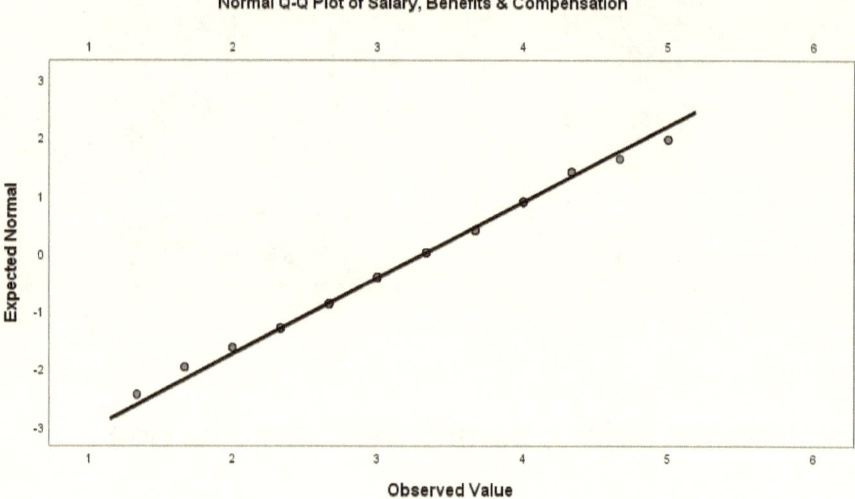

Normal Q-Q Plot of Salary, Benefits & Compensation

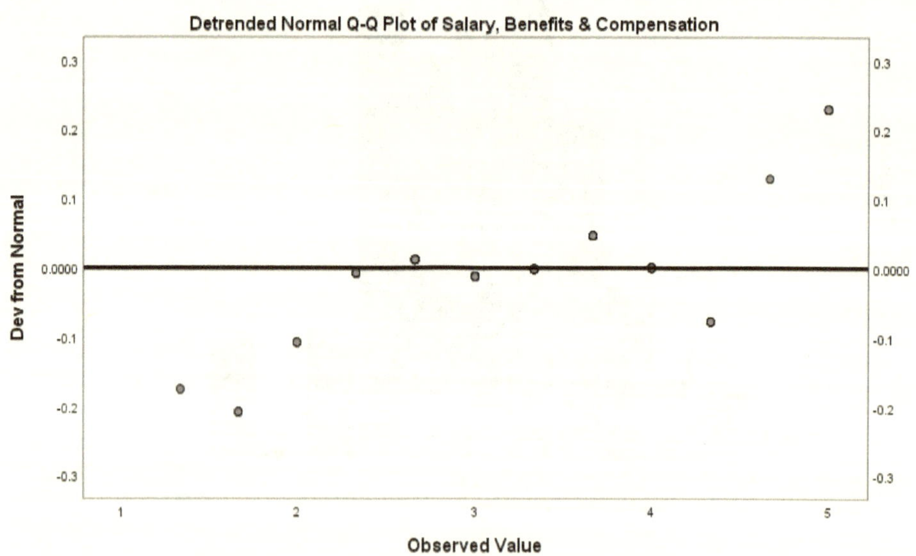

Detrended Normal Q-Q Plot of Salary, Benefits & Compensation

Variable: Work Environment

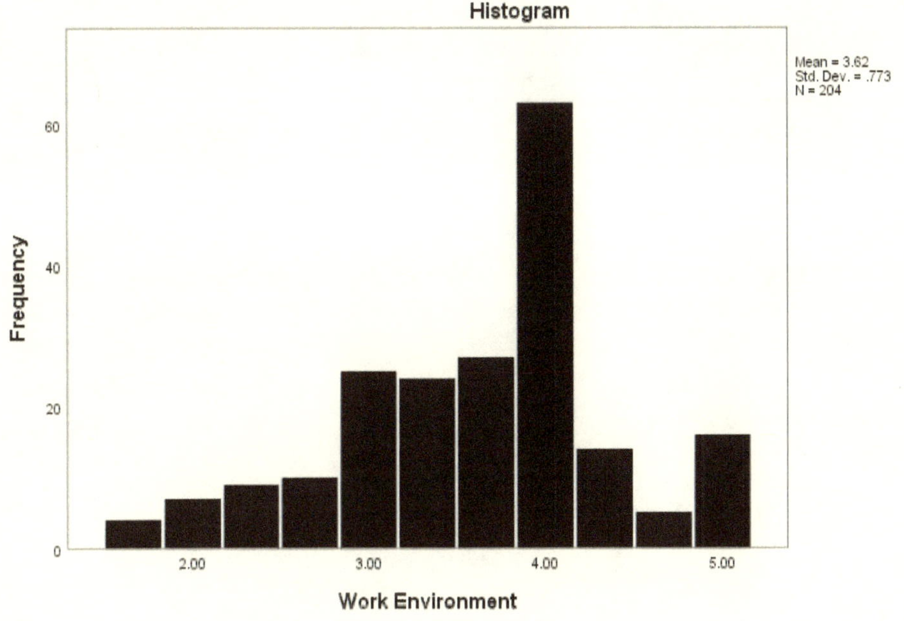

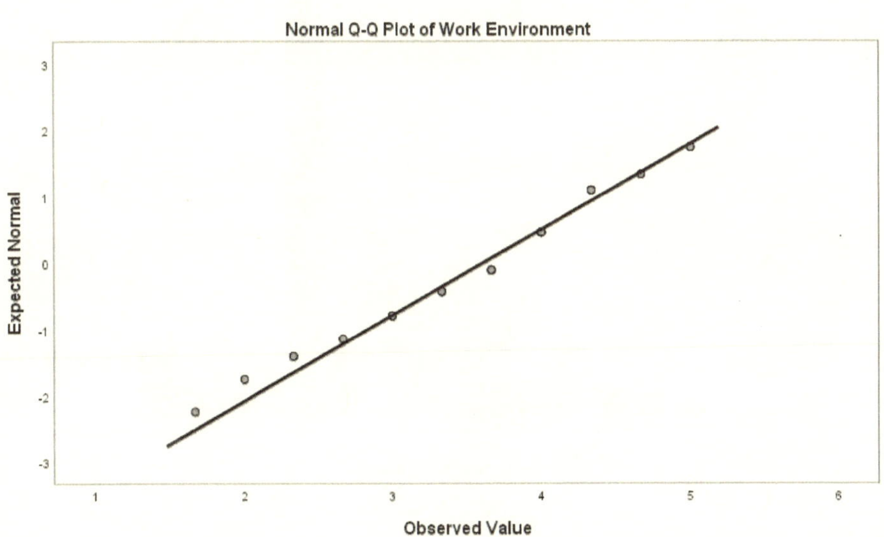

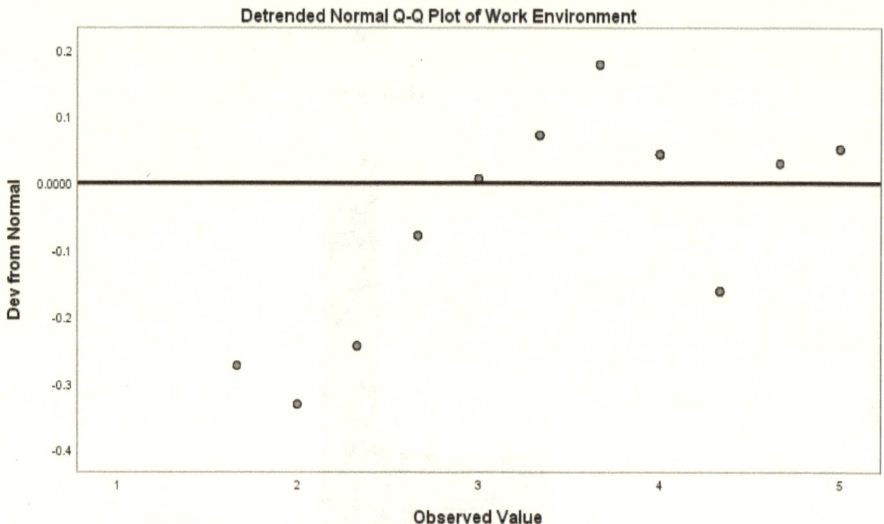

Variable: Employee Engagement

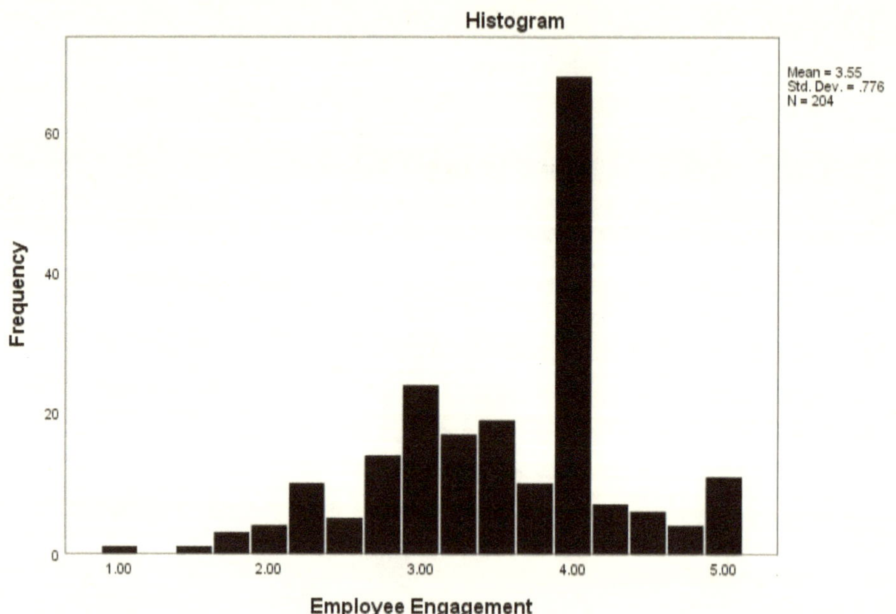

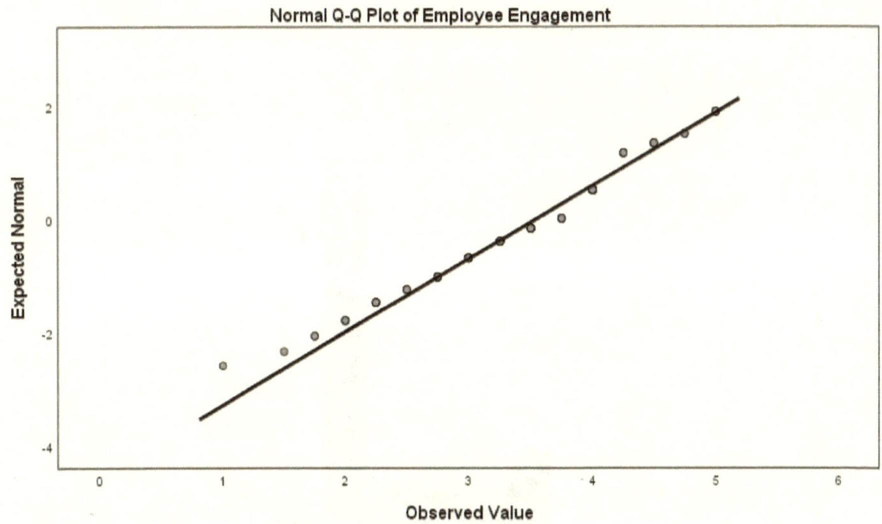

Normal Q-Q Plot of Employee Engagement
Expected Normal
2
0
-2
-4
0 1 2 3 4 5 6
Observed Value

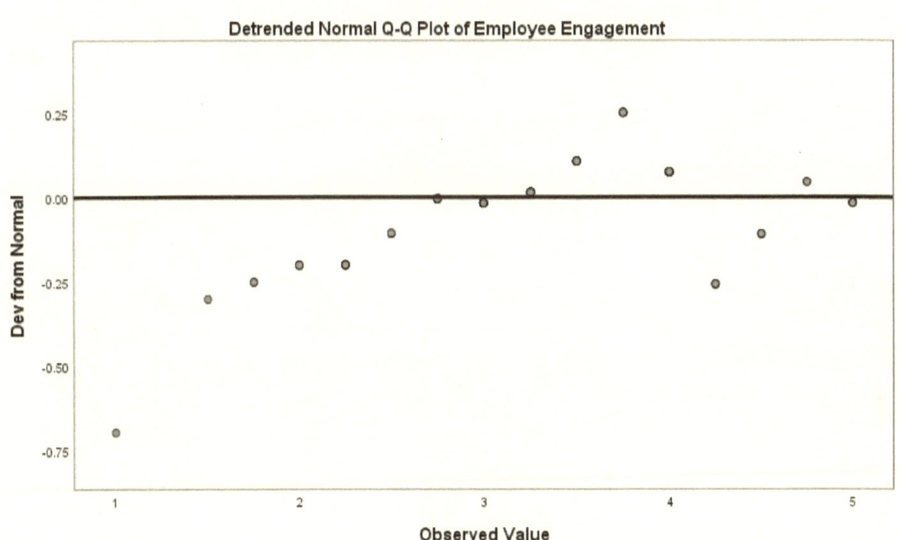

Detrended Normal Q-Q Plot of Employee Engagement
Dev from Normal
0.25
0.00
-0.25
-0.50
-0.75
1 2 3 4 5
Observed Value

Variable: Leadership Style

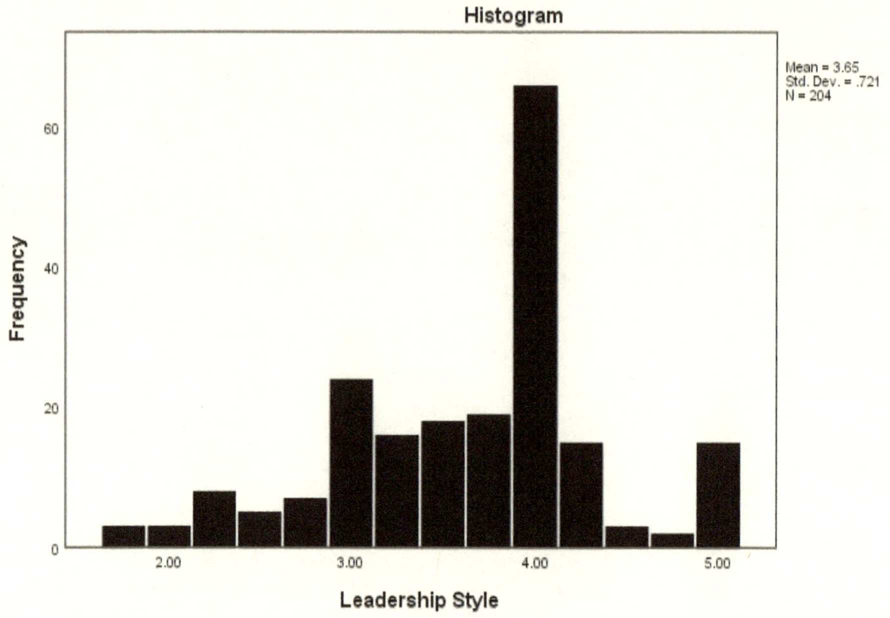

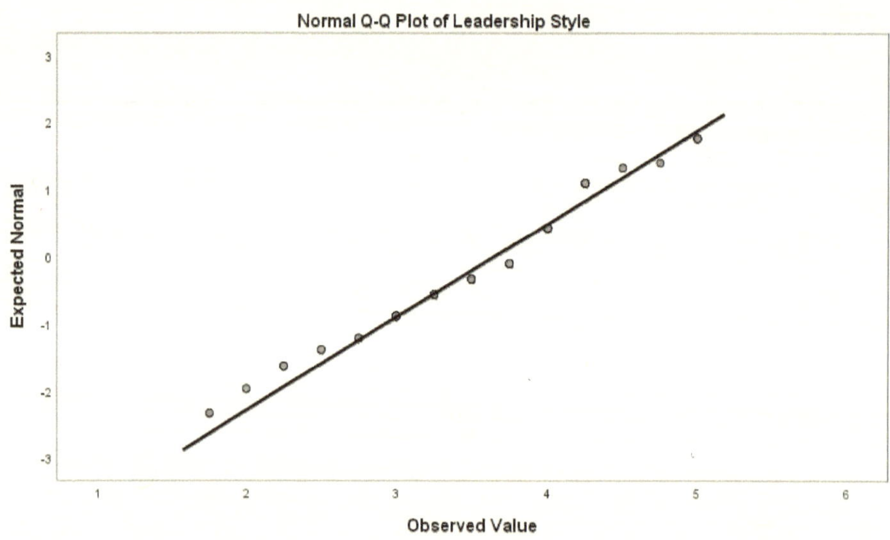

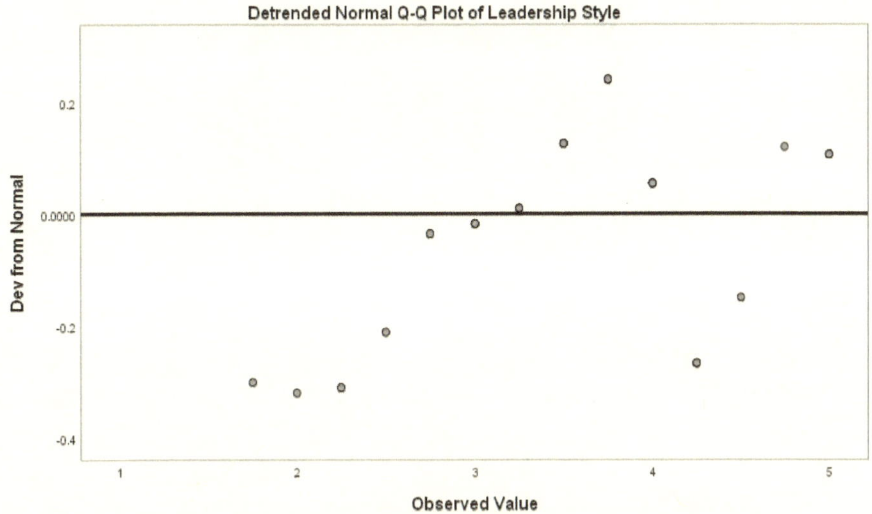

Variable: Training and Development

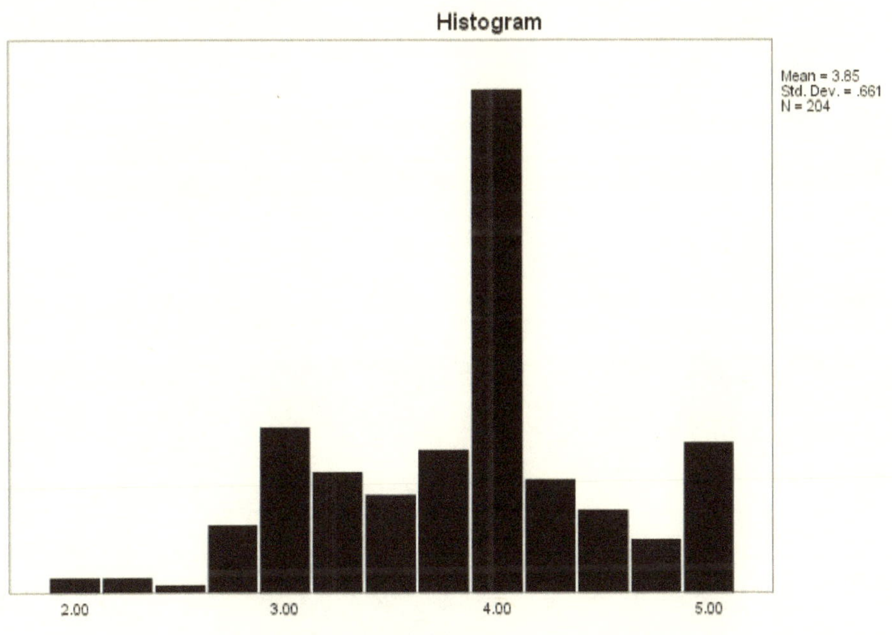

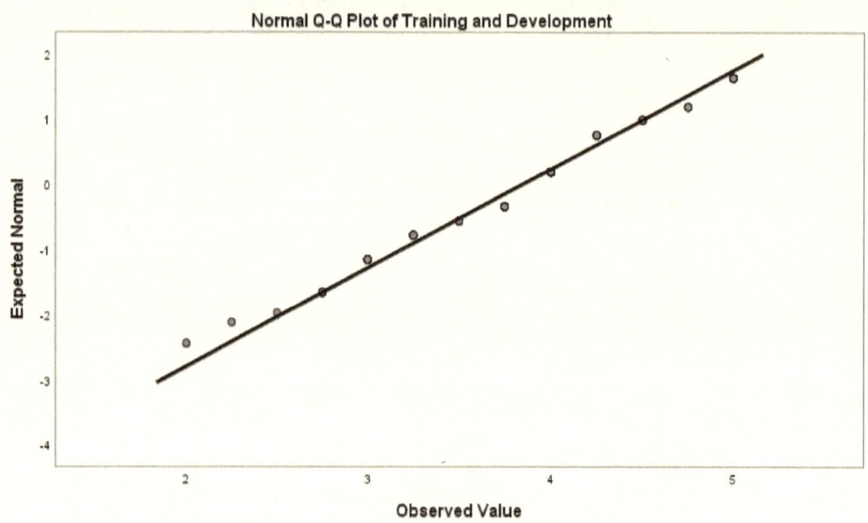

Normal Q-Q Plot of Training and Development

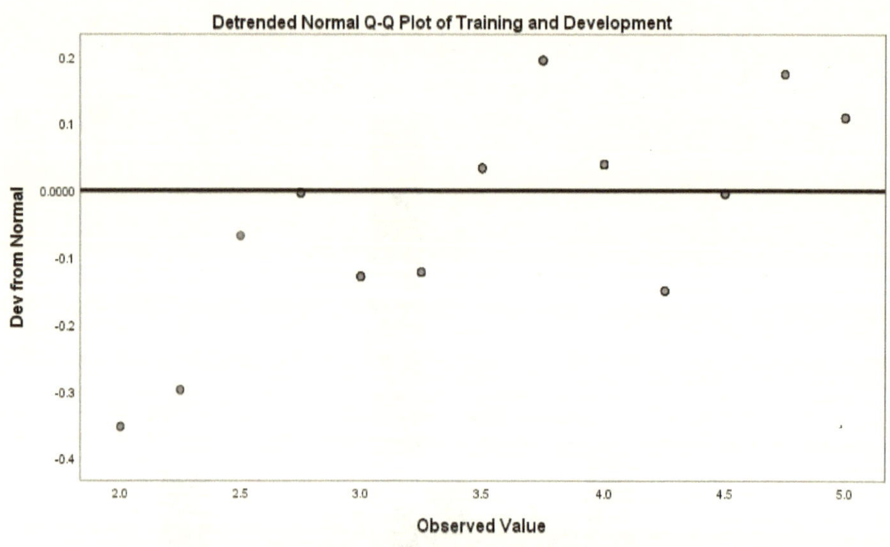

Detrended Normal Q-Q Plot of Training and Development

Variable: Intention to Implement Modern Manager's Coaching Skill

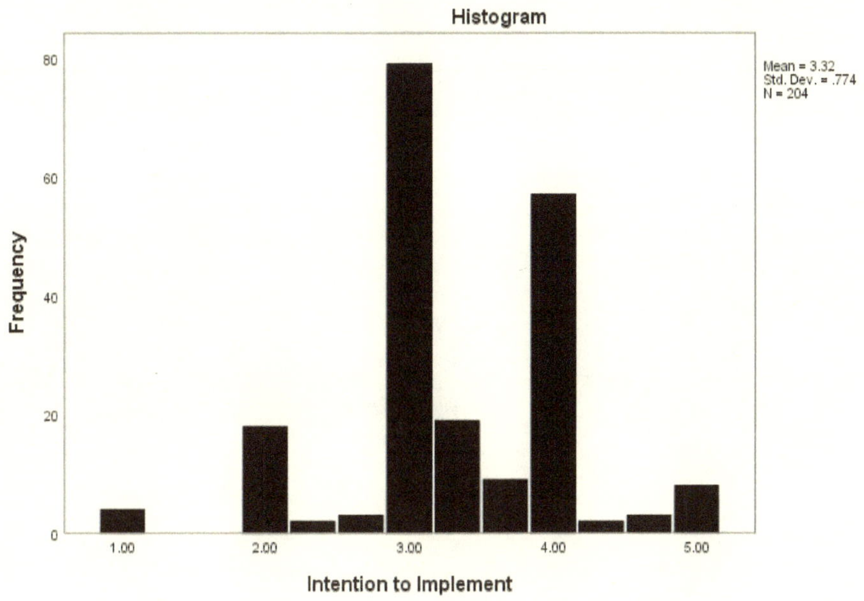

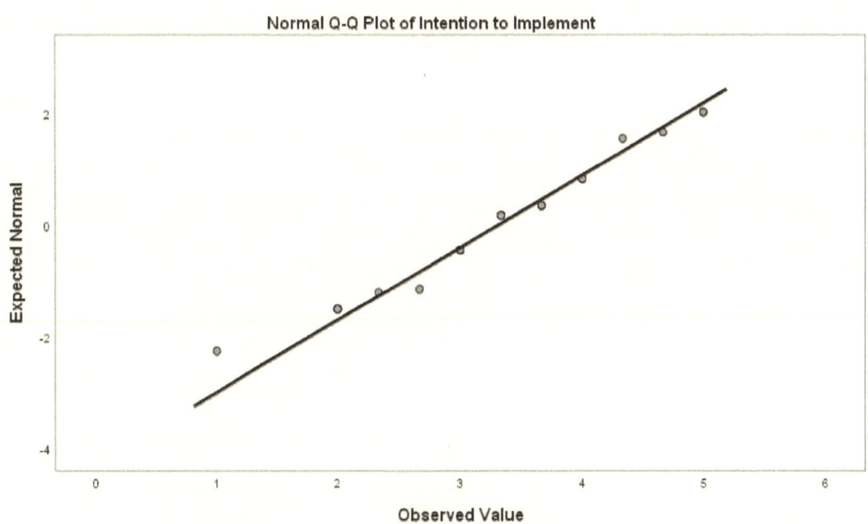

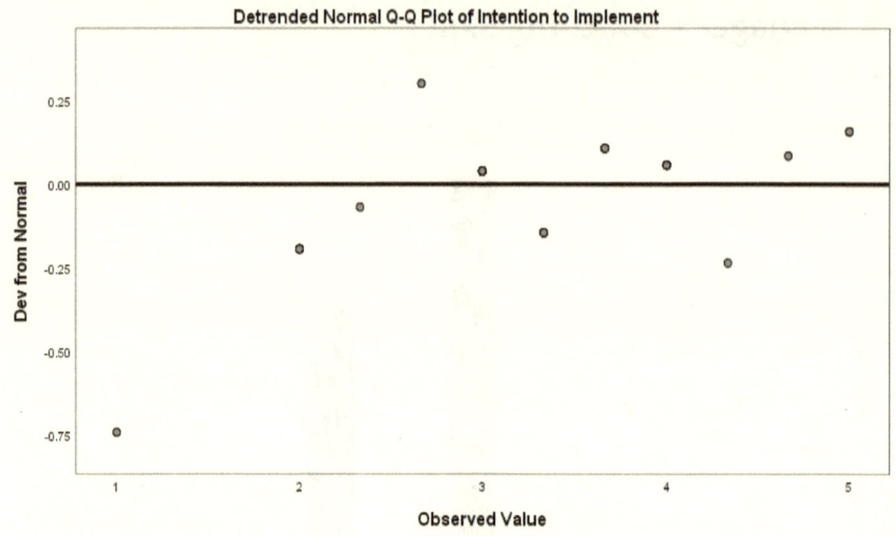
Detrended Normal Q-Q Plot of Intention to Implement
Dev from Normal
0.25
0.00
-0.25
-0.50
-0.75
1
2
3
4
5
Observed Value

Reliability, Mean, and Standard Deviation for Each Constructs

Variable: Salary, Benefits & Compensation

Reliability Statistics		
Cronbach's Alpha	Cronbach's Alpha Based on Standardized Items	N of Items
.756	.769	3

Item Statistics	Mean	Std. Deviation	N
I am satisfied with the existing company's compensation system.	3.60	.803	204
I think that the salary system of my company good enough to prevent me from searching for another job.	3.31	.931	204
I think that the purpose of single compensation system good enough to motivate employee.	3.06	1.037	204

Variable: Work Environment

Reliability Statistics		
Cronbach's Alpha	Cronbach's Alpha Based on Standardized Items	N of Items
.844	.845	3

Item Statistics	Mean	Std. Deviation	N
I think that my company having high quality work environment.	3.54	.867	204
My company provides me with career growth opportunities.	3.76	.862	204
I am satisfied with the current work environment at my company.	3.55	.927	204

Variable: Employee Engagement

Reliability Statistics		
Cronbach's Alpha	Cronbach's Alpha Based on Standardized Items	N of Items
.907	.908	4

Item Statistics	Mean	Std. Deviation	N
My company provides employee-centred internal programs for enhancing employee engagement.	3.55	.900	204
My company engages employees in career development and planning discussions.	3.50	.907	204
My company provides adequate support for employees.	3.63	.818	204

My company's management provide regular feedback for the employees.	3.50	.879	204

Variable: Leadership Style

Reliability Statistics		
Cronbach's Alpha	Cronbach's Alpha Based on Standardized Items	N of Items
.898	.899	4

Item Statistics

	Mean	Std. Deviation	N
Leaders in my company protect the team when faced with critical situations.	3.72	.785	204
Company's management make efforts for talent retention part of the core business strategy.	3.60	.827	204
Leaders in my company are flexible in adapting, understanding, and recognizing personal views and needs.	3.63	.898	204
Leaders in my company provide strategies that impact company performance and employee retention.	3.66	.781	204

Variable: Training and Development

Reliability Statistics		
Cronbach's Alpha	Cronbach's Alpha Based on Standardized Items	N of Items
.860	.861	4

Item Statistics	Mean	Std. Deviation	N
My company provide coaching or training to employees for enhancing their skills.	3.87	.802	204
My company implements effective development and training in my company.	3.68	.844	204
My company provides the required training and essential skills to employees.	3.81	.726	204
Training and development have an impact on employee retention.	4.03	.775	204

Variable: Intention to Implement Modern Manager's Coaching Skill

Reliability Statistics		
Cronbach's Alpha	Cronbach's Alpha Based on Standardized Items	N of Items
.961	.961	3

Item Statistics	Mean	Std. Deviation	N
I have already planned precisely what I will do as my first step to implementing Modern Manager's Coaching Skill in my company.	3.38	.800	204
I have already planned precisely when to engage in my first step to implementing Modern Manager's Coaching Skill in my company.	3.29	.814	204
I have already planned precisely where to engage in my first step to implementing Modern Manager's Coaching Skill in my company.	3.28	.797	204

www.ingramcontent.com/pod-product-compliance
Lightning Source LLC
Chambersburg PA
CBHW022002150726
47990CB00002B/559